WALTHER SCHEIDIG

Rembrandt's Drawings

ENGLISH TEXT BY
MARGARET PLAYLE
FOR MANY YEARS EDITORIAL ASSISTANT
OF "THE LISTENER"

BOSTON BOOK & ART SHOP, INC.

BOSTON, MASSACHUSETTS

"It is not enough to have a good mind, the most important thing is to use it properly. The greatest souls are capable of the greatest vice as well as the greatest virtue."

DESCARTES

Contents

The admirable selection of Rembrandt's drawings in this book is preceded by Dr. Scheidig's scholarly and enlightening introduction that would seem to need no introduction to itself. There is, however, one point of terminology that is of the very greatest importance to the appreciation of Rembrandt's art and which can, I think, be usefully explained to those who read no German and are not specialists. Since Dr. Scheidig has included in his text short accounts of Dutch art in the seventeenth century and of Rembrandt's life, I presume that his intention was to address an intelligent general public rather than specialists and it is with the same intention that I make this note. It concerns the full significance of the word *malerisch*.

The author of the English text has naturally enough translated this, initially, as "painterly" and in doing so has not missed the nuances of meaning inherant in the word "malerisch." In the passage where he discusses Plate 96, Dr. Scheidig uses the phrase *malerisch gezeichnet* which implies the existence of something called 'painterly drawing.' This awkwardness goes back to the great Swiss art-historian, Heinrich Wölfflin, who gave a special sense to *malerisch* that is now universally accepted by art-historians. It had to begin with a double sense which 'painterly' does not include. The translator of his *Kunstgeschichtliche Grundbegriffe* (Principles of Art History, 1932) said in a footnote that *malerisch* has "two distinct meanings, one objective, a quality residing in the object, the other subjective, a mode of apprehension and creation." The word 'picturesque' corresponds most nearly to the first of these but it is the second I hope to elucidate.

In the book I have just mentioned, Wölfflin expounded the two modes of apprehension and creation that have dominated art throughout its history in terms of the Renaissance and the Baroque. He based this on five polarities. Only the first concerns us at present: it is the opposition of the linear to the painterly. By 'linear' he did not mean only line drawing but a mode in which all forms, painted or drawn, are enclosed in a firm and continuous outline. This isolates and defines each object as a distinct mental concept. There is no better or more extreme statement of this mode than the often-quoted passage from Blake's *Descriptive Catalogue*:

> The Great and golden rule of art, as well as of life, is this; That the more distinct, sharp, and wiry the bounding line, the more perfect the work of art ... How do we distinguish the oak from the beech, the horse from the ox, but by the bounding outline? ... What is it that distinguishes honesty from knavery, but the hard and wiry line of rectitude and certainty in the actions and intentions? (Keynes ed. 1957, p. 585)

This almost mystical and certainly moral passion for the linear sufficiently explains Blake's persistent praise of Raphael, Michelangelo and Dürer and his violent abuse of Rembrandt, Rubens, Titian and Correggio. It is their 'blotting and blurring' which we now call the painterly mode. Wölfflin's prolonged examination of this can be summarised as a mode of seeing in areas rather than edges, areas of tone and colour which are emancipated from the bounding outline. They frequently merge almost imperceptibly into one another, but they may also, as very frequently in the drawings which follow, be juxtaposed in sharp contrast of light and dark. If, as an example, we look at the tree on the extreme right of Plate 106 we can find bits of edges, as it were, but the trunk *as a whole* is not bounded by outline and it exists primarily as a very dark area flanked and even penetrated by very light areas. It is of this emphasis on areas by strong tonal contrasts that Dr. Scheidig is speaking in the passage which started me on this discussion. *Das farbige Eigenleben alter Mauern und das Spiel von Licht und Schatten in den tiefen Doppeltoren ist nie zuvor so wahrhaft malerisch gezeichnet worden.*

By the use of the word *farbige*, Dr. Scheidig has even gone so far as to suggest that such tonal contrasts may imply colour for, although it can mean 'tint' our first reaction is to read it as meaning 'colour.' This is a sort of metaphorical usage, as we speak of colour in music. Since colour and light are really inseparable this merely emphasises that the painterly mode is one of areas rather than edges.

This mode of depiction is not merely an artist's technical device. It corresponds to a whole specific way of apprehending the external world. In the painterly, as Wölfflin said, "nothing whatsoever coincides with the form which we think we know in life." Which we *think* we know... Thinking is a process of intellectual apprehension which does not correspond with the sensuous apprehension of a visible object. We can *think* of a square-topped table with equal legs and even think we can see it but in fact we cannot. It is perspective and the incidence of light which determine what we see – the top never square, the legs never equal, the edges never absolute. The painterly apprehension grasps this pure visual experience with all its distortions, uncertainties and discontinuities. The painterly creation presents this: it records an impression, not an object.

The distinction between the painterly and the linear is further confused by the fact, which Rembrandt's drawings amply demonstrate, that the painterly may be achieved with lines. But these lines do not make a direct statement of forms but convey them through their creation of light and dark areas. In Plate 1, for example, the line on the left of the collar is broken to suggest its flexibility, though the collar itself *as we think of it* is bounded by a continuous line. The line on the right of it is so thick as to become an area in itself and its function is to help establish the interplay of light and dark. These lines and all Rembrandt's indeed have an entirely different function from those in a drawing by Blake or Ingres. The lines in Plate 2 while primarily establishing the areas do also mostly correspond in direction with the forms: they run up and down the verticals, across the horizontals and therefore to that extent perform a linear function. But in the later drawings – Plates 95, 124A, 132 or 160, for good examples – though this correspondence may occur in some passages it is by no means consistent. Horizontal lines may darken a vertical surface and vice versa. This independence of the line becomes almost complete in such drawings as Plate 33, 44 or 143; and in the latest drawings is manifested in dark and measurable statements which approach abstraction. What defining function *as line* remains in Plates 168 or 173? We arrive then at the paradox that a painting by Raphael, which contains no single drawn line, can be called linear and a drawing by Rembrandt, composed entirely of lines, can be called painterly.

That Rembrandt was an extreme example of the painterly does not, of course, account for his personality as an artist nor for his greatness. I have only tried to clarify one element in his mode of apprehension and creation. What he expressed through this, what, in fact, was significant in his forms, can be appreciated in this book by the contemplation of the drawings and with the help of the author's exposition.

Anthony Bertram M. A. (Oxon.)

Seventeenth-century Netherlands culture, of which Rembrandt is the supreme representative, is a minor miracle in the history of Western development.

Until about the end of the sixteenth century there were only "Netherland Provinces," which formed neither a political, administrative nor linguistic unit. A few decades later, however, the Dutch Republic had come into being and had established itself as a Power to be reckoned with in European politics. It was now active in world trade, enjoyed a flourishing domestic economy, and had developed an individuality in the fine arts, particularly in painting, which thrived like a natural growth among the hothouse plants of Court and Catholic art.

No explanation for this miraculous achievement was to be found in the country itself. Marshy lowlands had been formed by the alluvial deposits in the Rhine and Maas deltas; the violent incursion of the North Sea into the Zuyder Zee clearly showed the danger constantly threatening the flat land with its sandhills on the west coast. Land was valueless. No trade routes of any importance ran through the Lowlands. Ocean shipping from Rotterdam and Amsterdam operated within narrow boundaries, plying chiefly between the Netherlands and the Scandinavian and Baltic countries. There can be only one explanation for the coming of the Golden Age to the young Republic: the character of its people and the skill with which they made the structure of their land serve the political situation of the day.

Netherlanders have waged battle with water for centuries. With dunes and dykes they have kept the sea at bay. With canals they have prevented swamps from forming and the land from being flooded by the tributaries of the large rivers. It was an inspiration to use the constant coastal winds as sources of power, and by means of hundreds and hundreds of windmills to drain the soil and make it serviceable. Thus, in this small territory, a system of canals and locks was constructed and brought great benefits. The land was drained and irrigated; even the smallest piece of land was surrounded by canals. For trade, these canals offered as it were a network of highways incomparably more closely woven than that of any other country. With boats and small ships the canals ensured a convenient means of transport, even for the heaviest loads, to every village and every farmstead. All the inhabitants were in touch with one another and could easily make use of the wider communications afforded by the Rhine, the Maas and the Schelde. This close connection brought about an equal distribution of the fruits of labour and prevented the formation of barren areas or districts of over-supply. Remembering that in the sixteenth century in the Germanic countries a local bad harvest brought misery to thousands because the transportation of bulk commodities such as corn was impossible over long distances on the country roads of that time, one can imagine what extraordinary benefits the artificial canal and

12

sluice system conferred on the Netherlands. No highwaymen could bar the roads to plunder or demand ransom, because not just one canal led from town to town, but there was a choice of a dozen little byways. In times of war the canals with their locks made the land into an almost impregnable fortress. When life was at stake the sluices could be opened and large areas of land flooded to prevent invasion or the advance of an army.

Politically, jurisdiction of the Netherlands had since the Middle Ages belonged to the Holy Roman Empire of the German nations and the whole country was under imperial rule. Imperial Stadholders represented the rulers; nevertheless the cities and country towns possessed such considerable privileges that they were more independent than the majority of German towns, which were ruled by princes. There developed in the Netherlands a civic culture which had its origin in the Guilds and Corporations. Add to that the fact that in the Netherland Provinces the Catholic Church had for many years exercised no authority through bishoprics, monasteries and land-ownership, that knights (later robber-knights) were of no great importance. Thus about the middle of the sixteenth century the Provinces presented a picture of a quite incomparable social organism for those days. Conflict between the towns was hardly likely because of their proximity one to the other and because of the easy communication by numerous canals. Medieval Guild rules ensured equality between craftsmen. Medieval collective thought still ruled the town merchants, allowed them to trade in "companies" and prevented the rise of individual wealthy, and therefore powerful, houses. Peasants and fishermen were, as in other countries, without rights, but even the peasants in the Netherlands could at that time collectively gain free possession of new land from the sea or marshlands. The fishermen, with their boats, could make use of the canals and sell their catches direct to consumers, and so, on the basis of the new society, were in a better position than fishermen in neighbouring countries. The great German Peasants War that started with the uprising in Wesel and spread to the frontiers did not take a hold in the Netherlands Provinces.

Everything changed when the Emperor Charles V abdicated in 1556, proclaiming himself bankrupt and his plans for a Middle and West European central rule a failure. He handed over the Empire to his brother Ferdinand of Austria and the Spanish throne with sovereignty of the Netherland Provinces to his son, Philip II. From his court in Madrid the new ruler tried to carry through reforms in the Netherlands by modernising and centralising administration at the expense of the medieval guild and company organisation and against self government in the towns and estates. At the same time the Papacy, whose stronghold the Spanish Court had become, began the re-catholicization of the Netherlands, with an attendant heresy hunt. A network of church properties was to be spread over the land. The old bishopric of Utrecht was to be made into an archbishopric, a newly appointed archbishop was given Mechlen as a residence, fifteen new sees were founded, and were provided with land and retainers, so that the bishops might replace the usurped autonomony of the states as the new rulers of the land.   13

The revolution that now broke out against the Spanish rulers had two aspects. In politics a conservative faction were opposed to the ideas of the Spanish royal house which aimed at a strengthening of the central power and on the union of the two main administrative bodies. On the confessional front the Netherlanders fought quite simply against the barbarism of the Spanish inquisition and the betrayal of non-Catholics to King Philip II by a highly placed Spanish priest. It was impossible to hand over fifty thousand heretics and rebels for trial or to intimidate them with threats of chains and execution, but two thousand would be near the mark of those betrayed.

By the Treaty of Geneva, 1576, all the Netherland Provinces joined to wage war against the Spaniards; nevertheless, three years later the Spanish Stadholder Don Juan of Austria succeeded in bringing the southern, geographically less strongly protected, provinces to surrender, by means of treaties and the renewal of certain of their administrative privileges. The seven northern Provinces, which for the most part had adopted Calvanism, and whose canals, inland seas and swamps afforded greater protection, signed the Union of Utrecht in 1579 and declared themselves independent of Spain in 1581. The "miracle" of the Golden Age of the Netherlands (or Holland, as the new State was now named after the most important of its provinces) was perfected by the retention of revised medieval societies and administrative order on the one hand and on the other by freeing themselves from the Catholic priesthood and the control of thought by Catholic dogma.

The exemplary blossoming of industry, handcrafts, commerce and the fine arts was made possible by men who worked together in guilds, companies or municipalities, but who began to think independently each for himself freed from outworn dogma. Then, too, the phenomenon of the specialisation in Dutch art can be explained by the effect of the medieval restrictions governing activities combined with individual freedom of thought. While compulsory adherence to Guild rules had long been forgotten in Italy, while court art developed in France, Spain and also in Germany – in Prague, Munich and Dresden – the Dutch retained corporative control and through it medieval insistence on craft quality and priceworthiness. Specialisation ensured the best results and made it possible to control the standard, even in painting. If an artist painted only a still life with fruit, then the buyer and the Guild were able to recognise quite easily whether the picture was, comparatively, "good" or "bad." The giving of a commissioned work to a single painter or to various artists, as was customary in sixteenth- and seventeenth-century Netherlands and Holland, sprang from similar thought processes. A master of landscape would paint in the background, another specialist would fill in the main subject in the middle distance, a third the flowers in the foreground. On the other hand, the combined achievement of members of a workshop, society or guild was coupled with respect for the individually created masterpiece.

The form of government which came into being with the Declaration of Independence in 1581 was curious. It was a union of sovereign provinces without centralised power and without

14

a common law, which, however, retained the office of "royal" Stadholder as an old established form of government. The young republic discarded outward ceremonies that had been observed for about a hundred years. Meanwhile states that were striving towards centralisation and absolutism warred against one another. Holland, freed by the truce with Spain, gained greatly from this situation. In the wars between Spain, France and England, the head of Queen Mary Stuart fell in 1587; in 1588 the Spanish fleet was destroyed by England; in France the Huguenot wars raged in a struggle for central power, which was brought to an end by the entry of Henry IV into Paris in 1594. In Germany everyone fought everyone else; princes fought among themselves and against the states, Protestants in sects against each other and against catholicism, townsmen against peasants, artisans against tradesmen. And as a latent threat to Central Europe the frontier of Turkey stretched to the Plattensee in the neighbourhood of Graz.

The young Dutch Republic profited by this turmoil. Rich refugees came from the southern provinces that remained under Spanish domination. Antwerp withered – Amsterdam flourished. Dutch companies financed fleets for trade with the East Indies, with Central and North America, and ousted the Spanish and English merchants. Riches flowed into the country and through guilds, corporations and business houses were divided fairly equitably between tradesmen, artisans, seamen and other workers. In 1596 the Spanish royal house, whose wars had been financed by German and Italian capitalists, became bankrupt. The "Fugger" withdrew as money lenders to Emperors and Kings, and in their place the Bourse of Amsterdam – a Dutch corporation – became the centre of the European gold market.

From 1600 till the middle of the century Holland was paramount in trade and the foundation of its overseas commerce was laid. North and South America, South Africa, India and the South Sea Islands were opened up to Dutch commerce. Typically Dutch was the founding of the West Indian Trading Company. Five provinces contributed considerable capital and gained in return a voice in the administration. A representative of the States-General, the less powerful partner in central government, became its director. Profit from trade with the West Indies flowed unceasingly into the provinces and thence to private money lenders.

Religious freedom, which the Dutch had won in the War of Independence, resulted in greater tolerance, and Holland became an asylum for men who had suffered because of their religious principles. That is not a contradiction of the fact that the political power of the States-General – which wanted to open the door to every sect and faith, even the Catholic counter-reformation and the Jesuits – was overthrown in 1618, and the Grand Pensionary of Holland, Oldenbarneveldt, was executed the following year. The realisation that militant-intolerant views against tolerance had not been overthrown, allowed of no other solution. Where, however, no struggle for power was bound up with a religious ideology then Jews, Catholics, Mennonites and Lutherans could carry on their religious observances undisturbed, and live according to the tenets of their belief. It will always remain a title of honour of the Dutch people that witches were 15 hunted out and put to death for the last time in 1595, while in Germany the last witch was burnt in Würzburg in 1749.

One of the first tasks undertaken by the cultural awakening of the Dutch was to replace medieval dogma by new knowledge and research. No university had so far been founded in the territory of the seven northern provinces, but even before the beginning of the War of Independence the protestant Stadholder William of Nassau-Orange, in 1575, had founded the University of Leiden, with the approval and from the coffers of Holland and Zeeland. It was typical of Holland that other provinces also founded universities in Utrecht, Amsterdam, Groningen, Franecker and Harderwyk, and as a result four universities – Leiden, Amsterdam, Franecker and Harderwyk – were little more than 30 miles apart.

The world-famous Dutch paper industry had its beginning at this time. Printing works and publishing houses sprang up. Printers and publishers who had fled from Antwerp carried on their work in Holland. Soon their fame for accuracy and beauty equalled that of the Venetians in the sixteenth century. Scholarship gained much from the prevailing tolerance, which attracted learned men from other lands to Holland. The French philosopher Descartes, who had emigrated to Amsterdam, comments: "Because here everyone thinks only of himself and his business interests, the man who has no connection with business and trade can live quite unnoticed in freedom." The undertone of blame in the philosopher's praise touches on another trend typical of Dutch life in the "Golden Age." That each thought only of himself was an erroneous conclusion on the part of Descartes who did not understand the corporate feeling of Dutch society. Care for others – the old, the sick, orphans, the mentally deranged – was not an individual but a co-operative concern of Dutch people. A glance at the famous Dutch group portraits shows the manner in which such tasks were carried out. The earliest group pictures are of Crusaders, and showed participants in the pilgrimages to the Holy Sepulchre which came to an end with the spread of the Reformation in 1541. In their place, even as early as 1525, the defence pictures represented the voluntary town corps which in the struggle for freedom and the retention of ancient privileges, quite literally represented the shock troops. In the seventeenth century come the group portraits of representative Sydics and charitable organisations. In 1603 studies of anatomy were painted for the first time, and from then onwards the whole range of Dutch corporations and their representatives appeared in group portraits: corporations, Guilds, almshouses, *orphanages*, homes for refugees and the sick show their presidents (male or female). No other country at that time could boast of so comprehensive a welfare service as Holland, which however always took the impersonal form of a foundation, set up, supervised and maintained by voluntary contributions. Naturally individual people may often have said, "It's the business of the corporation to which I subscribe to care for the sick, aged or unfortunate, so there's no need for me to trouble about the old widow over the road." It could also be

considered a kind of welfare service when the Dutch people used their wealth to conserve their own blood in civil wars. There was no lack of wealthy German princes and noblemen who were quite ready, in return for good gold, to put their soldiers at the service of the States-General.

On the whole, however, the pursuit of personal luxury and the use of wealth for the achievement of power was restricted in Holland. By 1618 Calvanism had become the "church of the state," but not the State Church. The puritanical background of this form of religion still kept — even in the Golden Age — the churches bare, with clean whitewashed walls. Its adherents retained black and white for festival dress, and condemned processions, pageants, plays and folk festivities. The main trends of absolutism and baroque art to be found elsewhere, gained no acceptance in Holland until about the middle of the seventeenth century. When the town hall of Amsterdam, the richest city in Europe, was rebuilt after it had been burnt down in 1652, its architecture was much less ornate than that of castles built about the same time in German Duoezfürsten, Weißenfels or Gotha.

It was in those years of wealth on the one hand and puritanical restrictions on the other, that the foundation of Dutch customs was laid. Their characteristics can still be recognised in the importance attached to high quality in materials, in painful cleanliness and lack of ostentation of any kind. The commercial use of pure gold, so making capital "work," led to association with the jewellery trade where the surplus of gold could be put to good use and which offered the greatest possible concentration of material worth in the smallest object. The tulip "racket" of the years 1630/1637 was perhaps the most extraordinary example of how riches could be rendered harmless. At that time a tulip bulb of the variety "Vieroy" was listed at 5,600 guilders in a merchant's catalogue, and thousands of guilders changed hands from day to day on the tulip 'change for bills of exchange on tulip bulbs — not even for the bulbs themselves.

By the middle of the century, however, the zenith of the industrial boom had passed. The Treaty of Munster in 1648 brought formal recognition of independence from the German Empire and from the rule of the Spanish royal house. However, only two years later danger threatened the Republic, which now, as before, had a Stadholder: it seemed that they might lose their newly won freedom to a prince. The Stadholder William II of Nassau-Orange marched on Amsterdam, because the town demanded the disbandment of his costly land army which, since they had gained their freedom, had became superfluous. To protect themselves against their own Stadholder, the people of Amsterdam had to open their own sluices, pierce their own dykes, and flood their own lands. It was only with the death of William II in the same year that the peculiar office of Stadholder fell into disuse.

In England Charles I was beheaded in 1649 and the English Commonwealth was founded. The country, rent for centuries by dynastic wars, grew visibly stronger, and threatened the flourishing Dutch trade and sea power. The Navigation Act of 1651, by which the English forbade other nationalities from transhipping any goods other than their own, sought to cripple the Dutch merchant shipping and commercial trade, and led to the English-Dutch naval war   17 of 1652/1654. The defeat of Holland, the loss of a mighty battle fleet and numerous merchant vessels led to a severe depression in the commercial life of the young republic. Thus after about thirty years Holland's pre-eminence in world trade came to an end.

Side by side with science and ethnology, painting had played an important role in the commercial and cultural achievements in this period of the Republic. The people of the Netherlands had always delighted in pictures. Since the fifteenth century artists had educated their fellow-countrymen in the realities of space, light and colour. Pictorial art played an important role in daily life. Netherlanders were convinced of the influence that artists could exercise on the community by their thought and work, and had acknowledged this, if only in a primitive-distorted manner, when, in the great "picture-storm" of 1566, religious pictures were hidden in public buildings and private houses. After the storm had passed and the young republic was consolidated by the truce with Spain in 1609, the bare walls were a special invitation to artistic achievement. The Dutch could not take advantage of the opportunity where victory over catholicism had been final. The cult of the Virgin, the worship of the Christ Child, Madonnas, saints or miracle-workers were no longer subjects for painting, just as hero-worship of princes and noblemen, popery and priesthood were banned. Dutch painters had not only to create new pictures; they had also to find new subjects for pictures.

The artists, belonging to the people and to the artisan class, did not have to seek long for new material. They went with the stream at the beginning of the seventeenth century, which, concerned with humanity, led to humanistic themes in art. The Dutch for the most part concentrated, so far as painting was concerned, on politics, their own life, their small land and its native customs. They considered these more important than Ovid's "Metamorphoses" and the arcadies of the bucolics. They painted themselves as artisans, farmers, fishermen, seamen and merchants, with their daily small joys and sufferings. They painted their surroundings with flowers, meadows, cattle, dunes and seashore. The gardener wanted to find his plot of land in the picture, the peasant his poultry yard in painting. To the seaman a faithful representation of the safe return of his sailing ship after a long voyage was welcome. The Corporations played their part in this, when they made known their wishes by commissioning group portraits to decorate the walls of their town halls and board rooms, and to form a pictorial chronicle.

The demand for paintings during the first half of the seventeenth century seems to have been tremendous. There were however many artists ready and willing to meet these wishes in an exemplary and masterly fashion, under Guild control and intense specialisation.

The art world at that time was both modest and realistic. The painters were unaware of the pride of a higher calling. No romantic aura surrounded their work. Nevertheless, their achievements were respected and considered as important as the fruits of research, a good ship or a reliable clock. Paintings served as securities, as payment for a house; they were produced in series for re-sale in markets and at fairs, and they were sold on stalls and in booths. On the basis of creation, the painter enjoyed an expanding art trade: there were auctions, speculations in pictures, and, of course, there were also frauds. When we remember the close connection between town and country which Holland owed to the close network of canals, then it becomes understandable that the passion for pictures, as also art dealing, was by no means a perogative of the town-burghers. Probates of village worthies of the seventeeth century often include several dozen paintings by well-known artists.

The note in John Evelyn's Diary about his visit to the Rotterdam Fair in 1641 is well known. "The reason for the number of pictures (which were on sale at the Fair) and their cheapness is to be found in the people's lack of land for investment, so it is quite common for a simple peasant to pay two or three thousand pounds for pictures. Their houses are full of them. They re-sell them at their yearly markets at a great profit."

Rembrandt Harmensz van Rijn took part in this overwhelming art life from his fourteenth year onwards. He was the fifth of six children of the miller Harmen Gerritsz. Van Rijn and his wife, the baker's daughter, Neeltje Willemsd. van Zuytbroueck. As tradespeople, his parents profited by the growing wealth of the free country. Since 1589 the father had been halfowner of a mill in Leiden with a small newly built house belonging to it worth 1,800 guilders. By 1601 he owned five-eights of the mill; he bought the remaining half of a garden just outside the gate of the city, and he offered – though without success – 1,400 guilders for another house. He died in 1630, leaving everything he possessed to his wife, and when she died ten years later, the four surviving children inherited about 10,000 guilders.

With their growing prosperity the parents wanted one of their sons to become a scholar. Why Rembrandt, born on July 15th, 1606, should have been chosen is not known. Perhaps he had seemed more thoughtful than the others in his childhood. At all events his parents sent him to the Latin school, the preparatory school for the University, which he attended for seven years. On May 20th, 1620, in his fourteenth year, he matriculated (stud. litt.) and was enrolled in Leiden University. His entry at such an early age is not surprising; the University at that time provided, as its name implies, a large part of the general education and schooling in thought, which only later was provided by grammar schools. The earliest biography of the artist states that this education was to prepare Rembrandt for responsible work with the municipality – an administrative legal function. Very soon Rembrandt turned from this course, and became apprenticed to a painter, Jacob Isaacksz. van Swanenburch in his home town. It has already been said that painters were still organised in Guilds. The rights, duties and customs for which the Dutch had fought against the Spanish kingdom were strictly observed, especially in the early days of the Republic. Rembrandt could therefore only become an apprentice with the approval of his parents, and presumably he lived in his master's house. No drawings made by Rembrandt during his childhood have survived. Nevertheless he must have made some, and they must have convinced his family that he had the ability, inclination and application that fitted him for an artistic career.

Little is known of works by the painter Swanenburch, Rembrandt's master. It is certain, however, that the young van Rijn was given the solid and fundamental training prescribed and supervised by the Guild. In 1624, in Rembrandt's eighteenth year, the apprenticeship came to an end. As from childhood, so also from these years of training we have no works by Rembrandt. The drawings and studies he would himself have destroyed later; the paintings, carefully completed under the direction of Swanenburch, carried, as was then the custom, either no signature or the signature of the master, who regarded them as his own property and could sell them.

In a description of Rembrandt's home-town of Leiden, published in 1641, the Mayor said that already as a youth, during and after his apprenticeship, art-lovers had been amazed at Rembrandt's work. It was for this reason that his father had sent him to finish his education under the famous painter Lastman in Amsterdam. This also is a tribute to his parents understanding. They did not consider, as other tradesmen and artisans were apt to do, that their son had received all the training necessary, but they made it possible, certainly at no small cost, for him to continue his education in the great city of Amsterdam.

For half a year Rembrandt worked with Lastman as a pupil, not as an apprentice, and then, when he was nineteen, in 1625, he returned to Leiden. As Rembrandt's later life and work show, the family and the familiar home surroundings were for him a necessary source of energy. His parents' house, his sister and his brothers were all added incentives to his return.

He could now consider himself an independent artist, and so he rented a studio away from his parents' home. He shared it with Jan Lievens, who had also been brought up in Leiden. Although Lievens was a year younger than Rembrandt, he had been painting longer because he had not attended the Latin school. He, too, had been taught by Peter Lastman, but his tuition had ended in 1621, four years before Rembrandt's. There was no teacher-pupil relationship between the two young artists; they were friends who worked on similar tasks. In 1628 a note in a report on painters refers to Rembrandt as "highly esteemed, but precocious," which implied that he showed remarkable talent, but that this should not be over-rated for the time being.

However, a few years later the two young artists achieved fame far beyond their home town. Constantine Huygens, Secretary to the Dutch Stadholder, Prince Frederick Henry of Orange, paid them a visit. Constantine Huygens, father of the famous physicist, was the foremost representative of the young Dutch intelligentsia. He was highly educated, corresponded in several languages, wrote poetry tolerably well, had some knowledge of physics, astronomy, theology and philosophy, and in disposition showed the finest traits of the Dutch character: a love of simplicity, the homeland and its freedom. He was well acquainted with the practitioners of contemporary fine arts, his position as secretary to a statesman gave him a wide horizon. He wrote at length in his autobiography about the two young painters in Leiden. He had, he said, seldom seen such industry and perseverance; the painters were so absorbed in their work that they rejected the innocent pleasures suited to their age. He praised Rembrandt particularly for the way in which he portrayed emotions and for the grandeur of invention in his pictorial compositions. Huygens, who also knew Rubens and Italian painters of the time, regretted that the two young men did not want to study in Italy and had said that they had no time to spare for that. Huygens did not praise the painters publicly in 1631 – his autobiographical notes were for his own use and for his family.

While he was still in Leiden sharing the studio with Lievens the twenty-two-year-old Rembrandt took his first pupil. Gerard Dou was fifteen years old when he came to Rembrandt and he had already painted glass with his father. Two other pupils of the Leiden days, Isaac de Jouderville and Jacques des Rousseaux, are now known only by name, while Dou later became a highly esteemed artist of the Rembrandt School. From then on until about 1661 there was no break in the chain of pupils. Aert de Gelder seems to have been the last. He adopted the glowing colours of Rembrandt's late work and included them in charming paintings until well into the eighteenth century.

Rembrandt must have been a fascinating teacher, though a bad one insofar as he practically stripped his pupils of all individuality as long as they were studying with him. Only this can explain the fact that many drawings and some paintings exist which, after years of research and examination, cannot definitely be attributed to Rembrandt or to one of his pupils. That there is any doubt seems to contradict the idea of Rembrandt as a unique genius. Only the presumption that there was a temporary transference of genius from the master to a devoted pupil during apprenticeship makes the uncertainty concerning some of the works of the Rembrandt circle understandable. As, however, relatively few of the pupils' drawings which have been preserved bear corrections definitely recognisable as Rembrandt's, and there are a great number of copies of Rembrandt's original drawings made by pupils, it can be concluded that Rembrandt used his own drawings as models for composition, movement or expression, but corrected orally rather than with a pencil. The copies were kept by the pupils as material for study, and later they often made paintings from them, that is, based on Rembrandt's compositions. Unlike Rubens, Rembrandt does not seem to have employed assistants. Attempts to pronounce this or that part of Rembrandt's paintings as the work of assistants have so far not been convincing. Indeed, signatures on etchings and paintings make it clear that Rembrandt did not like to have his work confused with that of any other artists. In 1635, at the peak of his fame, he scratched on three etched plates: "Retouched by Rembrandt." On a painting made in 1636 he has written: "Altered and overpainted by Rembrandt." Also, the inventory of his art possessions indicates that eight paintings have been re-touched or overpainted by him. Doubtless these pictures bore corresponding inscriptions by Rembrandt. This procedure shows the feeling of responsibility that the artist had towards his work. He exercised his right to sell for his own profit paintings by his pupils, but he made it quite clear when he had in fact altered or overpainted them. This explains why in expert circles the idea of workshop production is not entertained where Rembrandt is concerned.

So far as we can judge from records, Rembrandt was an unusually businesslike teacher. He adhered to the guild rules, charged the customary fees for tuition, sold his pupils' paintings, as was his right, and received from four to fifteen florins for them. On the other hand, his pupils do not seem to have lived in his house, at least from 1639 onwards, so they were certainly not exploited as houseboys, kitchen hands or children's "nurses." In none of the legal cases, the reports of which are our main source of knowledge of Rembrandt's public life, did pupils come forward as witnesses for or against Rembrandt, as would have been probable had they been part of the household. It is true that apprentices bid in Rembrandt's name at art auctions and were present when their master gave his opinion on works of art. So when Rembrandt from time to time was by-passed by his pupils, it was apparently not because of any diminution in his fame as a painter, but because of the objectivity of his teaching and his lenient, unpretentious attitude. Outstanding artists emerged from his teaching. Several of them realised the fascination of the master and complained how difficult it was to discard Rembrandt's methods of painting.

Because of the close connection between all Dutch towns, to which we have already referred, Rembrandt's fame soon spread from Leiden to Amsterdam, which is indeed only about 25 miles away. Commissions, particularly for portraits, came more and more frequently from Amsterdam, and the artist must certainly have had to travel there to see the clients. Such journeys became so frequent that he finally, at the end of 1631, moved to Amsterdam.

The death of his father in April 1630 and of his eldest brother in September 1631 may well have made this separation from his family easier to bear.

Rembrandt went to live with the art dealer Hendrik van Ulenborch, with whom he had lodged previously. In June 1631 Rembrandt lent the dealer 1,000 florins, which he could spare even at the age of twenty-five.

The final impetus for this move, however, was probably the commission from the Surgeons' Guild of Amsterdam for a portrait of the guild members with their dean, Dr. Tulp, to be hung in the Guild House. Well established, renowned specialists in group portraiture, like Keyser and Elias, were passed over in favour of the young man from Leiden. From this time on the artist signed his work with only his Christian name "Rembrandt": he could now be sure that he would not be confused with any other painter with the same name.

While at Ulenborch's house he got to know the art dealer's cousin, Saskia, and became betrothed to her in 1633. A year later they married. Saskia was the daughter of a former mayor of the north Netherlands university town of Leuwarden. This marriage may well have been considered below Saskia's station in life in Leuwarden where her father was an alderman, but not in Amsterdam where Rembrandt was a renowned artist, and was also a past student of the Latin school and University of Leiden. Then, too, Saskia's relatives did not belong to the most exclusive circles. Two of her brothers were lawyers, one was an army officer, a brother-in-law was an artist — a painter of portraits and historical subjects — and so belonged to the same profession as Rembrandt; — another a town clerk, and another a professor of theology.

Years of domestic happiness followed for Rembrandt and Saskia, saddened, it is true, by the deaths of the three children born in 1635, 1638 and 1640. Rembrandt enjoyed the wealth that his work brought him. He showered costly gifts on Saskia, and attended numerous art auctions   23 in Amsterdam. He was both a buyer and a collector. In these years immeasurable wealth poured into Holland and so to Amsterdam, and Rembrandt shared in the prosperity. He speculated like others, but wisely: not in tulip bulbs, but in his own works, and by dealing in old paintings and works of other masters. Through Constantine Huygens he received a commission from Prince Frederick Henry of Orange, the Dutch Stadholder, first for three and then for two more large paintings showing scenes from the life of Christ.

A steady income encouraged him to expand his household. During the first years after his marriage he had continued to live in the art dealer Ulenborch's house where he had a flat. In 1639 he rented a house of his own. In this same year he bought the splendid house in Breestraat, for the high price of 13,000 silver guilders. Rembrandt paid scarcely a quarter of the cost in cash, and the outstanding debt led later to financial disaster. The income from the paintings ordered for the Stadholder proved far from adequate. Rembrandt had to bargain, and bestow "favours" on "middle men" to obtain payment. Constantin Huygens received a present of a very large painting, about 9 ft. by 7 ft. Rembrandt's instructions for the hanging of this picture in von Huygens' house were that it should be in bright light and in a position where it could be viewed from a good distance. It is at one and the same time the crudest, yet the most colourful and dynamic picture that Rembrandt painted: "The Blinding of Samson" (State Museum, Frankfurt). In view of its size the value of the painting was very high, but it is questionable whether, on account of its subject, it would have been saleable. For the tax collector Uitenboggaert Rembrandt did an etched portrait – "The Goldweigher" – in which he used all his artistic power to show the influential official's zest in his collecting and careful administration. Then in February 1639 Rembrandt received his money for the Stadholder's commission, altogether 3,044 golden guilders for the five paintings.

Rembrandt and Saskia found no happiness in their new home. On July 29th, 1640 they had a second daughter, whom they christened Cornelia, the name of their child who had died two years earlier. This other Cornelia lived only for two years.

The death of his mother, who was buried on September 14th 1640, in Leiden, must also have been a great blow to Rembrandt. We can be sure that there was a close tie between mother and son from the many portraits which he painted of her.

The joy that came to Rembrandt and Saskia in September 1641 with the birth of their son Titus was dearly paid for by Saskia's subsequent illness. On June 5th 1642 Saskia drew up her last will, and died nine days later. Rembrandt was left alone with his ten month old son. He had no mother, no sister, no kindly sister-in-law to help him.

True, the Mayor of Leiden had named him, in his town records, as the most famous painter of the century. True, Charles I of England possessed two of his paintings – a self-portrait and a portrait of his mother; but the mainspring of Rembrandt's happiness – his family, his home-life – was shattered.

It was in these years of bitter trial that he painted the picture with which his name will be forever linked, as Leonardo da Vinci's is with the "Mona Lisa" – Rembrandt's "Night Watch." Like the "Anatomy Lesson of Dr. Tulp" this was a corporation picture, commissioned by the volunteer defence corps of Amsterdam for the great hall of their newly built guildhouse. Besides Rembrandt, Joachim van Sandrart, Govert Flinck, Nicolas Eliasz, Jacob Backer and Bartholomäus van der Helst had received commissions. Each was to paint a different company of the corps, and in addition Flinck was to paint a group portrait of the four corps masters. Life-sized full-length portraits were required. Sandrart delivered the first painting in 1640, and Govert Flinck the last in 1645. Although the huge pictures hung together in one hall, they bore no relationship to one another, but as a whole they harmonised – all but Rembrandt's work. With this one exception, they were alike in that all the men were individually recognisable in the full glory of their uniforms, weapons, decorations and accessories, and all looked straight out from the canvas at the spectator. In contrast, Rembrandt had painted his as an action picture, as he had done for the "Anatomy Lesson of Dr. Tulp." His troop are just "falling in" for a sortie and are in the disorder that always precedes a march. We do not know whether the picture met with approval or not. Rembrandt received 1,600 guilders for it, and it hung in the guild hall with the others until after 1715. What has been written about adverse contemporary criticism, about the disappointment of the people included in the picture, the withholding of payment, and the withdrawal of the picture from the hall and its replacement by a picture by van der Helst – who had in fact painted another company – is just modern literary fiction. One can well imagine, however, that Rembrandt in his loneliness had become more unsociable and less inclined to adapt his own views on work he had undertaken to the wishes of his clients.

Yet another factor may now have made itself felt for the first time. Rembrandt's Amsterdam pupils had meanwhile become independent. They painted "almost" like Rembrandt, but they were probably more amenable to clients' wishes than was their former master. Ferdinand Bol, who had been a pupil of Rembrandt's since about 1632, was by 1640 renowned as an excellent portrait painter. Govert Flinck had studied under Rembrandt from 1632 until 1645; now he received a commission from the civil defence organisation on equal terms with Rembrandt. The really fashionable painter at that time was, however, Bartholomäus van der Helst. His "Company of Andreas Bicker" stood out in the hall because of its superficial brilliance and of the flattering likeness to the men of the guard. Helst, of whose education nothing is known, fulfilled his commission later than Rembrandt. He had not attempted to animate and dramatise "The Night Watch," but he had livened up disconnected groups of figures, above all, with more than a dozen pairs of haughty eyes levelled at the spectator. That he afterwards became the fashionable painter shows how shrewdly he had assessed the sitters in his flattering Guildhouse portrait.

In 1645 Rembrandt's household at last received a new centre of life after Saskia's death when Hendrickje Stoffels came to it. There were still unhappy disputes with little Titus' nurse, the

25

trumpeter's widow, Geertje Dircx, who now saw herself ousted and accused Rembrandt in 1649 of breaking the promise of marriage she alleged he had made. In 1650 she was put into a mental home, at the instigation of her relatives. Hendrickje Stoffels became mother to little Titus and wife to Rembrandt, though there was no formal marriage. The obstacle lay in Saskia's will, in which she had left her considerable estate, part of which had been Rembrandt's, to her son Titus, with the proviso that Rembrandt should have the use of it so long as he did not remarry.

In contemporary documents Rembrandt was still described as the "world famous" painter, and his paintings nearly always brought the highest prices at auctions. In 1646 the Stadholder Frederick Henry of Orange, shortly before he died, again paid Rembrandt 2,400 gold guilders for two more paintings of the childhood of Christ. But after this Rembrandt too began to feel the effects of the depression in the Dutch economy which followed defeat in the first Anglo-Dutch war at sea. There was still another reason for Rembrandt's increasing financial difficulties, for a falling income fewer commissions. His European reputation was growing, but in Amsterdam he was already "out of fashion" as a portrait painter. Between 1630 and 1645 Rembrandt had painted his own and the older generation. Now the younger patrons turned to younger painters, above all to Rembrandt's pupils. The main source of Rembrandt's income – commissions for portraits – became more and more precarious. It is not for us to call the younger generation of Dutchmen philistines unable to recognise Rembrandt's genius. Because he would not alter his own taste, as a portrait painter Rembrandt became a victim to the continually changing tastes of the bourgeoisie and their preference for the court painters – Rubens, Van Dyck, Velasquez, – who remained loyal to the declining princedom.

From 1652 onwards financial difficulties are clearly recognisable. In 1653 Rembrandt borrowed numerous large sums of money. Also, since 1649 he had paid no interest on the mortgage which encumbered his expensive house in the Breestraat. There were household cares too. In 1654 the Church Council of Amsterdam accused Rembrandt's housekeeper, Hendrickje Stoffels, of living in sin with the painter; they summoned her to an act of atonement in church and banned her from Holy Communion. Three months later she bore Rembrandt a daughter who, again, was named Cornelia. As though that were not enough, Rembrandt had difficulties connected with his art.

A Portuguese dealer, Diego Andrada, in Amsterdam abruptly terminated, through a notary, an apparently verbal commission. Andrada demanded that the portrait of a young girl should be altered because, he claimed, it was not a good likeness. Failing alteration, Rembrandt should take back the portrait and waive the fee. Rembrandt would not agree to these conditions. He demanded payment in full, when he would finish the picture and submit it to the judgment of the professional body, the jury-foreman of the St. Luke's Guild. Then he would alter it or not according to their verdict. Although we do not know the outcome of this conflict, nevertheless it throws light on the position of the artist who considered himself bound by higher principles of art than literal likeness in a portrait, but who was approached by clients who, more and more, wanted to be shown both as they were and beautiful.

In 1655 Rembrandt made his first effort to meet his financial difficulties by the sale of his costly art collection and his house, which he had bought at the peak of Holland's prosperity. He purchased another house, for which he paid 4,000 guilders in works of art – the half of the purchase price. As already six months later he could no longer call the house his own, this speculation seems to have been unsuccessful, though we do not know what works of art Rembrandt had given in payment. Even then Rembrandt had not sustained the full financial disaster. Pressure was put on him by his creditors to pay the main debt of 11,000 guilders on the large house in the Breestraat, and so in 1656 he had to declare himself bankrupt. Later generations have to thank this misfortune for the most meticulous inventory of his house and his fabulous collection of works of art and old and new treasures of Holland, the Netherlands, Italy and Germany.

All the walls of the great house were adorned with pictures, cupboards were full and tables were covered with old engravings, woodcuts, costly materials and curiosities. In 1658 the house was auctioned and realised almost the full amount of the purchase price. On the other hand, there was unfortunately a diminution of 5,000 guilders in the value of the art collection. This can only be explained by the economic depression in Holland, and particularly in Amsterdam, after the defeat of the Dutch fleet and the destruction of the merchant vessels. The total amount received from the sale did not suffice to pay Rembrandt's debts, and thereafter he was unable to trade for his own profit.

But Rembrandt's strong family feeling, which had passed on to Titus and Hendrickje Stoffels, came in this tragic situation to the rescue of the aging father, the seventeen-year-old son, the thirty-five-year-old housewife and her little daughter, Cornelia.

Titus had inherited his money from his mother Saskia and this could not and dared not be touched by Rembrandt's creditors. Titus had willed his possessions, at the time of his father's disaster, to his small half-sister Cornelia, had made his father guardian and had given him the usufruct of Cornelia's inheritance during his lifetime. With the money inherited by Titus from Saskia, amounting to 40,000 guilders, Titus and Hendrickje founded a business as art dealers, though it was of course Rembrandt who had the expert knowledge. Titus and Hendrickje even foresaw the possibility that Rembrandt's unsatisfied creditors might claim his future works of art, and they countered this danger so that he could continue his creative work undisturbed. In a carefully tho ught out agreement of 1660 they took Rembrandt into their business as expert adviser in return for his keep, and in consideration for past and future support he pledged all paintings (or money received for them) that he might from then on execute in their house. This legal document sounds gruesome: Rembrandt no longer possessed anything, could not in future earn anything for himself no matter how hard he worked, and would get in exchange board and lodging with his son and his housekeeper. For any other family such an agreement would have been an absurdity, but here it worked wonderfully. Rembrandt was at last freed from debts, speculations and threatening bailiffs, and he was given the possibility of immersing himself much more deeply in his art. Moreover, from contemporary documents it does not seem as though Rembrandt lost the respect of his Amsterdam fellow-citizens by his financial disaster. It is most likely that in the commercial spirit and speculative zeal of the town inability to pay one's way was looked upon as a misfortune but not as an offence against propriety and morals.

Rembrandt received two important official commissions after 1660. One had a tragic outcome which robbed the world of a masterpiece of artistic creation, comparable to Leonardo's "Last Supper" or Grünewald's Isenheim altarpiece. The new City Hall, dedicated in 1655, lacked murals. From time to time commissions were given to painters of the high baroque school and also to pupils of Rembrandt. The town council specified as themes for these pictures scenes from the Old Testament and from Roman history which exemplified virtues, heroic deeds or unselfish acts. The pictures were subjected to severe criticism with special emphasis on modern treatment. Jan van Bronkhorst got his painting back in 1660: he was asked to alter it in accordance with the wishes of the town councillors and to accept a reduction of 800 guilders in his fee of 1,800 guilders.

So far Rembrandt had not received a commission. Then in 1659 the Princess Amelia of Solms announced that she would be making a state visit. In the Town Hall there were still large areas of the enormous walls unfilled. Lunettes on the way to the reception hall were empty! Now in the greatest haste Rembrandt's pupil Govert Flinck was commissioned to paint twelve pictures of tremendous size, which he began to design in November 1659. Scarcely three months later he died and left only a few designs. In the utmost embarrassment the town councillors divided the project. The Flemish painter Jacob Jordaens, the German Jürgen Ovens, Rembrandt's youth friend Jan Lievens, and finally Rembrandt himself received commissions. From the beginning of February 1660 to late July 1662 Rembrandt was engaged in painting the approximately 30 square metre picture from the past history of the land: the conspiracy of Julius Civilis with the Batavians against the Romans. He completed it successfully, and in a printed publication of July 21st, 1662, the monumental work was described in its place in the reception room of the Town Hall. What happened after that which led to the fragmentation of the great work is not clear. Already on August 28th, 1662, Rembrandt promised part of the payment to an art dealer who made a claim for alterations ordered by Rembrandt to the town hall picture. So it appears that alterations *were* necessary and Rembrandt was willing to make them. One may presume that the changes were occasioned by architectural considerations, but not by dissatisfaction with Rembrandt's achievement. In the latter case Rembrandt would certainly not have been prepared to make changes. Therefore there is no answer to the question why Rembrandt's painting was not put back in the same place. Moreover, the painter Jürgen Ovens received, on

28

January 2nd 1663 the whole 48 guilders for finishing in four days Govert Flinck's design of the same historical scene that Rembrandt had painted. This hurriedly completed work is still in the place which Rembrandt's monumental painting should have occupied. Rembrandt then tried to retrieve his five and a half by five and a half metre painting as a saleable object. He cut out the large main group and tried to make it into two roundels. Even this fragment (Stockholm, National Museum) suffices to show how great was the loss the cultural world suffered when Rembrandt's own contribution found no place in this great project.

At the same time that Rembrandt was working on this gigantic mural, he had to complete a second important commission. After an unfavourable verdict on Bartholomaus van der Helst's design, the Clothmakers' Guild of Amsterdam approached Rembrandt in 1661/62 for a group portrait of their Syndics who watched over the quality of the finished materials on behalf of their council. Rembrandt did not disappoint the Syndics. They received the most profound of all Dutch group portraits, in which the master showed that their authority and public image are only recognised when they have been gained by tolerant survey and impartial examination of the knowledge and purpose of others.

Just as with the "Night Watch," when Saskia fell ill and died, now Rembrandt painted these two great late works in a time of deep emotional distress. Hendrickje Stoffels, his housekeeper, the mother of his daughter Cornelia, and his "employer" since the business agreement was drawn up in 1660, made her will on August 7th 1661 "sick in body though still able to walk and stand." It is not known how long after that she died, but the sale of Saskia's grave in the Oude Kirk, which Rembrandt put through on October 27th, 1662, may be seen as a means of acquiring a grave for Hendrickje in the Westerkerk near his house.

Now Rembrandt was left alone with his 21-year-old son Titus, who had become a painter, and the eight-year-old Cornelia. As stipulated in Hendrickje's will, Titus continued to deal in works of art with his father's help, which, above all, ensured certainty in Rembrandt's life and creative work. To simplify his business management Titus was declared of age a year before it was legally necessary. The fact that Rembrandt offered 1,000 guilders for an alleged Holbein portrait speaks for the continuing prosperity of the business. When Titus married, in February 1668, Magdalena van Loon, whose parents had been friends of Rembrandt's for many years, Rembrandt could hope for a renewal of family life resulting from this connection and the marriage of the young couple; only seven months later he stood at his son's grave. He painted his daughter-in-law several times. There is no picture of his grandstepdaughter Titia, who was born in March 1669. As a wishful dream Rembrandt painted in his last great work of 1668 a happy family with three healthy children, the community which Rembrandt longed for but never experienced. Without loving care, presumably because the daughter-in-law was herself seriously ill, Rembrandt's life ended on October 4th, 1669. On October 8th he was buried in the Wester-kerk churchyard, where Henrickje Stoffels and his son Titus also rested. The funeral appears to have been worthily equipped, presumably by the Van Loon family; the memorial book speaks of sixteen coffin-bearers and records twenty or fifteen guilders as the cost. Saskia's burial cost eight guilders in 1642, his son Titus's ten guilders and ten stivers in 1668. How poor or how rich in worldly goods Rembrandt was when he died we do not know, because the inventory of his effects lists only personal possessions, while the art works and antiquities, which were displayed for inspection and sale in three rooms, were not listed but were sold privately.

The daughter-in-law, Magdalena, died thirteen days after Rembrandt. The codicil concerning the inheritance of the grandstepdaughter Titia permits the conclusion that Rembrandt at the time of his death owned property to the value of about 9,000 guilders. Rembrandt's daughter Cornelia married in 1670 the painter Cornelius Suythof and went with him in the same year to Batavia. They had a son whom they named after his grandfather Rembrandt.

Even before Rembrandt died the "Golden Age" had come to an end. The ease and freshness with which the painters of the young republic had portrayed it, its life, its ships, flowers, beer-houses, guardrooms and corporations were lost. In the seventeenth and eighteenth centuries the painters of Rembrandt's generation died: Ostade 1685, Terborch 1681, Jan Steen 1679, Isaak van Ruisdael 1682, Pieter de Hooch 1677, Vermeer 1675. The most important of Rembrandt's pupils died too: Lievens 1674, Dou 1675, Ferdinand Bol 1680, Govert Flinck 1660, Eeckhout 1674, Hoogstraaten 1678, Barent Fabricius 1673. The elements of medieval bourgeois culture in the striving for equality of the guilds, in corporative thinking and trading, favoured by general conditions, brought about the flowering of the "Rembrandt time" in Holland, But now these elements disappeared more and more under the overwhelming influence of absolute monarchism which now prevailed in countries bordering on Holland.

With the revival of the office of Stadholder in the year 1672, in the person of Prince William III of Orange who also became King of England in 1689, court life, with royal residences and princely households, came to Holland. Court taste won acceptance, the patricians withdrew themselves more and more from the burghers and craftsmen; they were subservient to the English-Dutch princedoms, and sought distinction through titles, arms and seignorial rights, and to win a place in the ruling power of absolutism. These tendencies were, however, completely alien to the world of Dutch art, and so after 1680 there was no longer any specifically Dutch art.

Is Rembrandt the draughtsman a different man from Rembrandt the artist, a painter whose canvases in Dresden, Casel, Leningrad or Paris make so deep an impression? Is this draughtsman other than the master-etcher of the beggars, Abraham's sacrifice, or the return of the prodigal son? A look at the drawings in general may make Rembrandt's achievement clearer. Whether an artist has made many or few drawings is no criterion of his ability. Where the remoter past is concerned one must take into account a very heavy loss of drawings, but, apart from favourable conditions of survival, it is possible to judge from what can still be seen whether an artist has drawn much or little. It is certainly no mere chance that we have no drawings by Rembrandt's contemporaries Velasquez and Frans Hals.

The Dutch in Rembrandt's day were enthusiastic draughtsmen. In their endeavours to represent in pictures the world around them, their own life and country, they studied and drew people, animals and landscapes with greater zest than their Italian, French and Spanish contemporaries. Rembrandt's day marks the first appearance of drawings produced not merely for practice and preparation but as works created expressly to be sold. They show all the characteristics of paintings so far as composition, execution and use of colour are concerned, and they are only superficially drawings because paper, as opposed to canvas, has been used when making the picture, and also because slow-drying oil-paints have been avoided. Bearing the clear signature of the artist, they are easily recognisable as cheap marketable goods.

Rembrandt shares with Leonardo da Vinci and Albrecht Dürer the distinction of having left the greatest wealth of drawings, but the character and purpose of the drawings differ completely in each master's work.

Leonardo da Vinci drew as an investigator. He first worked out clearly in his mind facts in nature or in mechanics, and then recorded them with perfect precision in his drawings. For Leonardo the creative experiment existed side by side with research and yet was closely linked with it. While he drew he reflected on the way in which nature "could have" taken on different shapes through over- or under-development of separate parts, as in the case of the human face. However, Leonardo could not fully express his conclusions in drawings alone. The explanatory word almost always accompanies his graphic observations, reflections and experiments. Apart from the direct preparations for paintings, murals or three-dimensional work, Leonardo's drawings are recorded results of research as unique as the artist himself.

Dürer's drawings, which are so emotionally moving, are far less powerful than Leonardo's works. Here we see artistic development: Dürer works on himself; he trains his eye to observe and his hand to good and ever better representation of what he has seen. Much more a craftsman 31 in the best sense, Dürer always had a mental image of the finished work as he drew. In drawing, he prepared a work of the highest possible achievement, in that he decided definitely on the composition and then studied the parts that seemed necessary to work it out. Drawings are made as preliminaries for portraits; landscape drawings become backgrounds for paintings; details of costume and armour such as he had seen in Italy enrich his mythological etchings. His paintings, etchings and woodcuts are, for Dürer, works of art. His drawings are exercises: by practising he prepared himself; by drawing he assembled the parts from which finally a work of art should grow. Of course Dürer also made sketches for their own sake, as mementoes, without any specific work in mind, but by far the greater number of his drawings were made to develop his talent and widen his experience in preparation for works of art other than drawings.

Rembrandt's position as a draughtsman can perhaps be made clear by saying that he thought graphically. If one defines thinking as silent inward speech and speech as audible thought, then Rembrandt's thought was an inward drawing and his drawing visible thought. When considering individual drawings it will be possible to indicate the train of thought that has found expression in the final drawing.

Naturally Rembrandt also drew to gain practice and to gather experience. Is it just by chance that we have today no drawings made during the years of his childhood or when he was studying under Swanenburch and Lastman? We would rather think that he destroyed them himself because this was work carried out under instruction and did not spring from his own thoughts.

Only a few of Rembrandt's drawings served as preparation for paintings or etchings. For the hundreds of his painted portraits there are scarcely more than a dozen "preliminary" drawings. Rembrandt never seems to have arranged an advance session in which he drew a head, as was usual, so that he could later paint the portrait without a sitting. In contrast to Dürer's, Rembrandt's drawings were not preliminaries to other works.

The connection between Rembrandt's thought processes and their delineation explains the rhythms in his output of drawings. Man's thought also has its rhythms: problems are tackled; considered for a time; then put on one side for a while. Thus for a number of years Rembrandt gave his whole attention to drawing country scenes in the neighbourhood of Amsterdam; then for a long time no more landscape drawings were made, since apparently his thoughts and mind had turned to other matters. A similar concentration can be seen for a short time in the drawings of nudes. In Rembrandt's studio his scholars must often have made sketches of nudes. There are very few drawings of this kind by Rembrandt himself until about 1655. Then, however, up to the time when the painter Rembrandt at length created the marvel of the Paris "Bathsheba," he drew female nudes, almost always with ensnaring sensual charm. If we consider that Rembrandt's thoughts and feelings were erotically excited during these years and regard these drawings as thought made visible, then their appearance at this period is understandable.

32

What has already been said about the drawings of the three artists, Leonardo da Vinci, Dürer and Rembrandt, and how different the approach of each artist was — can perhaps be made clearer if their drawings are considered side by side.

In his mural "The Battle of Alghiari" Leonardo wanted to paint furious horses. He imagined *Pl. A* what they would be like and drew them. But his comparative and morphological investigation led him further: He drew a second sketch of a raging lion and followed that with the profile of a man moved by anger (as only Leonardo would do as a matter of course at that time): in this way the question answered itself. The scientist Leonardo, who in his drawing recorded the results of his observations in the realms of morphology and anthropology, stands revealed in the sketch.

In 1521 Dürer made nine sketches, all on the same sheet of paper, of St. Christopher carrying *Pl. B* the Christ Child through the water. Each drawing is complete in itself, each of them made into a painting would be a perfect picture. Every one of the nine drawings is a finished piece of artwork. One might say that Dürer has based his drawings on a great wealth of knowledge, which enables him to make numerous variations of a single theme, and all are exemplary. But they are not variations, they have not been made as the result of thinking "around" or "further;" they are parallel expressions made possible by the richness of his craftsman's ability and knowledge.

Anticipating the main theme, let us take an example of Rembrandt's train of thought in art. *Pl. C* He set out to show a condemned man about to be beheaded. He drew the criminal on his way to the block, with the executioner by his side, a comforter and an escorting guard. His thoughts *Pl. D* run on, he rounds off the composition by adding more guards on the right, more spectators on the left. Now it has grown into a large scene, with almost too much display for the poor sinner. So in thought Rembrandt exalted him to Jesus by filling in the foreground with people from *Pl. E* the back before whom the Saviour has been placed for judgment. That the original condemned man and the executioner no longer fitted into the picture did not worry Rembrandt. For him the chain of thought was right; he saw this as the finished drawing.

One can find many examples of this meditation which for Rembrandt is synonimous with the drawing. Secondary ideas on the subject rise to the surface. Biblical scenes break in on everyday happenings. Everyday happenings appear suddenly in a bibilical context. Reflections of a formal nature thrust themselves to the surface and press into the picture. With Rembrandt's drawings we can really gain only from the originals themselves a glimpse into the changes in direction of Rembrandt's mind.

No comparison is possible between Leonardo, Dürer and Rembrandt, but Rembrandt probably comes nearest to self-contradictory thinking of modern days.

The trend of his thought reaches out to the spectator, the nuances of the drawings evoke further thought. Not that we have to disentangle confusion, or bring to a conclusion unfinished musings! Rembrandt has posed no riddles, but has again and again offered food for meditation on the subjects of humanity, love of one's neighbour, morals, as no other artist before or since has done in the west European world of culture.

It would scarcely be a mistake if, judging from the expression in his many self-portraits, one thought of Rembrandt as a very reserved and silent man, who was perhaps not used to discussing ideas. His method of communication was not the word, but the line. This makes it easier to understand the vast range of his drawings, even though these were not made as preliminaries to paintings or etchings.

We may take it for granted that the 1,500 drawings still extant are at the most only half of his actual output. When the painter Jan van Capelle died in 1680 — that is only eleven years after Rembrandt — he left in his collection of over 7,000 drawings some 500 by Rembrandt. Of those, about 135 are described as "Vrouvenleven," which could be loosely interpreted as "Woman's life and Children." Today we know of only about 60 to 70 drawings on this theme, that is only about half of those belonging to Cappelle. A cautious estimate points to a production of over 3,000 drawings, without taking into account the completely vanished drawings made during his childhood and in his student days.

Though reproductions of the drawings – even the best – seem irritatingly homogeneous, it is well worth considering Rembrandt's methods of drawing more closely. It is a fact that his drawings are often covered with numerous "corrections," but it would be wrong to think that these alterations rectify „mistakes." Rembrandt drew with so sure a hand from such an early age that he no longer made "mistakes." Carelessness, tentative suggestions of outlines, certainly, but nothing wrong. So when Rembrandt made alterations, redrew lines, changed shapes, or erased lines and replaced them by others, it was because his ideas had taken another direction and his pencil or whatever he was using must follow.

Rembrandt drew sometimes with pens, red or black chalk, but more frequently with liquid media which could be applied with fine quills or with coarse reed-pens, sometimes too with tools which often included stubby, worn-out paint brushes. He also used perfect brushes of various sizes to draw, to apply flat washes and to shade. The liquid media varied. Most often it was a dark brown water-colour called bistre, often, too, black water-colour: indian ink. He very rarely used ordinary ink as this attacked or soaked into the paper.

Many descriptions of his drawings in catalogues include a note saying "Correction in masking white," which indicates that parts of the drawing – that is to say, phases of Rembrandt's thought – have been hidden from sight because they have been overlaid with a relatively thicker water-colour. Rembrandt frequently did this. The effect is now confused where in the course of time the strong pigment used for the "hidden" drawing has seeped through the masking white, and can now be seen with equal intensity side by side with the upper layer where this remains intact.

Distinction must be made between this "masking white" and another use of white. Often when Rembrandt had just finished a brown or black drawing, he went over certain parts of it with a very fluid white. He thus blended the dark colour down to the exact tone of light brown or grey that he desired. In such cases layer is not superimposed upon layer; the watery white is used here not for alteration but as a definite technique. The "water brush" goes still further. Using this wet brush without any pigment Rembrandt goes over parts of the fresh drawing. He dissolves the brush strokes almost entirely with the water, they become softer, and give tone around the original line. This again is no change in the line of thought behind the picture, but a superb method of varying the emphasis of the strokes.

Finally one can say something about the "dry" quill-pen or "dry" brush. To get a particular effect, Rembrandt needed, especially for his later drawings, a line that was strong in colour and definite but at the same time flexible and not over-emphasised. He achieved this by loading his brush or quill-pen with thick, semi-dry water colour that flowed with difficulty and so produced   35 a broken line. The magic of Rembrandt's late drawings depends to a great extent on this technique. If one adds to the consideration of Rembrandt's methods of drawing the fact that accidental flecks are sometimes left standing, and are sometimes rubbed away with the finger, but that the superfluous colour from the blot can also be used in a most ingenious way by spreading it with finger or brush for toning a surface or for shading, then we have gained some small insight into the technique used for making the drawings, which explains their present, often confused and soiled condition.

So far as we can judge from the earliest drawings that have survived, Rembrandt had, as a matter of course, to conform to the ideas and methods of his teachers. When he first became independent in Leiden he drew from models as a preliminary to paintings, and his drawing media from about 1626 to 1630 were those then in general use in studios — red and black chalk.

But already in drawings like "The Archer with the Turban" one can detect his mind at work *Pl. 3* and follow the train of his thought while he draws. The archer has two bows. He carries one on his back; he holds the other in his right hand. In the first composition only the bow on the back was indicated. Then Rembrandt decided that he did not want the bow carried in this way; so he drew the right forearm with the hand grasping the bow which was now resting upright on the ground. He left the back part of the drawing as it was, though it no longer had any relevance. Rembrandt's heightened interest in area toning can clearly be seen in this drawing. He does not outline the figure with chalk. He shades in the body and the cast shadows, separates the back and left arm almost entirely by light and builds up the figure by concentrated yet seemingly careless strokes.

The drawing of an old man with arms outstretched is similar in execution. This has been *Pl. 4* hastily sketched from a model in the studio. The figure and its use in an etching of about 1629 — Peter healing the paralysed man at the gate of the Temple (Bartsch 95) — raises some doubts as to the meaning of the gesture. The old man's attitude in the drawing conveys a sense of deep sorrow. This is not at all suited to the subject of the etching, and yet Peter's attitude, as he speaks the miracle-working words to the paralysed man, is almost exactly the same as that shown in the drawing.

A number of paintings made during the early days in Leiden have as their subject old men sitting in gloomy rooms but illuminated by strong light which streams towards them diagonally from above. Rembrandt worked out this motif in such pictures as "Peter in Prison," "The Rescue of Peter from the Dungeon," "A Scholar Studying," "Two Philosophers in Discussion," and others. They stem from sketches of a white-haired, bearded old man whom Rembrandt drew in the light of the studio.

One drawing shows in profile the full figure of an old man seated. Rembrandt tinted the *Pl. 2* paper to a reddish tone — a middle value from which he could work towards both darker and lighter tones. In such drawings Rembrandt concerned himself with an artistic problem of the day. Some Dutch painters who, unlike Rembrandt and Lievens, had not refused to go to Italy to study had adopted a method of painting that accentuated the reality of the component parts of large compositions. Rembrandt's teacher Lastman painted in this way, and Rembrandt was

Pls. 3 & 4 familiar with the style from other pictures that came to Amsterdam. In his early drawings for paintings – in the Archer, and the Old Man with Book – Rembrandt endeavoured to capture the startling effect of light. He let the steep headlong shaft of light dissolve the shapes as they penetrated into them. (The light seems to engulf the object – it is the object itself that is dissolved, and only the shading and lines give the contour.)

But Rembrandt, from the beginning of his creative life, was more concerned with Man himself than with such artistic problems. He wanted to interpret man's features, his movements, his deeds, and to explain his shortcomings. Light and shade were welcome to give weight to the evidence.

Although Rembrandt painted and etched many dozens of self-portraits, drawn likenesses are *Pl. 1* rare. The brushwork self-portrait of about 1627/1628 shows clearly how Rembrandt succeeded in confronting himself as though he were a stranger. The open mouth speaks of complete objectivity. Light and darkness threaten to divide the body in two; in the mouth, in the eyebrows and in the neckcloth light thrusts its way vigorously as a force into the darkness. Rembrandt subdues all these contradictory details to composed unity through the power of the lustreless eyes.

Huygens says of the Rembrandt of these years that he had never seen such industry and perseverance. The young man did not even permit himself the innocent pleasures suited to his years; it was to be hoped that he would take more care of his not very strong body, which had already suffered.

From about 1630/31, when Rembrandt moved finally to Amsterdam, his drawings were seldom made merely as preliminaries to paintings and etchings. Definite studies from models came almost to an end. Rapid sketches took their place, single figures were grouped together and a relationship was established between them.

Pl. 5 A momentary impression is captured in the red chalk drawing of the "Polish Officer." Rembrandt attached great importance to hats, caps and turbans. In this case the costume interested him because the man owed his dignified appearance to the tall cap with the feather.

Pl. 7 For the sleeping woman – a badly damaged drawing in black chalk – the motif came to him unsought in his own home. It is typical of the way in which Rembrandt "interprets" in drawing at this time that he has left the face blank – without features, – has made the lower part of the figure appear immobile and calm by using broad parallel lines and flowing strokes, and in contrast has animated the upper part, where the beating of the heart and the breathing continue uninterrupted by sleep, by using divergent lines and wavy strokes.

A peculiarity of Dutch building, which later spread to the German North Sea and the Baltic coasts, was the hatch-door, Rembrandt often used it in drawings and etchings with a wealth of associated meanings. It is the house door giving on to the street, which is divided horizontally in the middle and can be opened as a whole or in part, the upper section forming a kind of

shutter. This door divides and connects. With only the upper half open the people who live in the house can take part in the life of the street; but at the same time they possess a kind of bulwark separating and protecting them from the outer world. The outer world: that, in Rembrandt's day in the cosmopolitan city of Amsterdam, was a turbulent street life with musicians, beggars and refugees whom the inhabitants enjoyed watching – and whom they no doubt helped with money and food – but always from within their own home and with the protecting half-door in front of them.

Thus Rembrandt caught the fleeting expression of curiosity mixed with distrust on the face *Pl. 6* of the bearded old man behind the hatch-door. Only the face is lit up in the semi-darkness of the entrance hall. Then Rembrandt pondered over the drawing. He heightened the hat to add dignity to the wearer. He created an illusion of space and air by toning the dark background with white. He blended the colour of the cloak over the left shoulder to a grey to give plasticity to the body. And lastly he added the tall begging box thrust over the half-door close to the old man's left arm.

In the street Rembrandt's attention was caught by the dissimilarity of two people walking *Pl. 9* together: a vivacious young woman, talking and gesticulating, was accompanied by an old man whose hat told all that need be known of intractability and decrepitude.

Another time he saw four Orientals in the street, perhaps they too were actors. Rembrandt *Pl. 10* has emphasised the pathetic exhortation of the man in the loose wrap by the daring sweep of the light turban just as he has emphasised the listlessness of the partner by the ill-shaped head-covering. Such drawings are of course the result of direct observation. Phantasy and thought have then worked on them, filling out the first impression and resulting in a considered work of art. Those to whom the drawing appears too hasty, the legs of the man on the right too plump, should remember that Rembrandt had at this time painted the "Anatomy Lesson of Dr. Tulp." Certainly what appeared important to Rembrandt was simply drawn in a masterly way. How then comes the harsh domineering look on the face of the man on the right? How do we know the dour obstinacy of the man on the left, without an eye, a mouth being drawn?

In just the same matter of fact way as he took home life, street-, market- or theatre-scenes and wove them into his drawings, so also Rembrandt took well-known national stories, texts from the Old and New Testaments and interpreted them in sketches. One must realise that the Bible stories, teaching and parables provided a field of thought familar to all Dutch people irrespective of social standing and education. Although Calvanism forbade religious pictures and left the whitewashed church walls bare, everyone knew the words of the Bible, and its exhortation to make use of its teaching in daily life to the service of God. Rembrandt invented nothing when he set the biblical happenings in the familiar Netherlandish scene. Pieter Breughel had already, in 1566, moved the Slaughter of the Innocents to a wintry Flemish village. Jan van Kalkar had transposed the Raising of Lazarus to a churchyard in the market place of a Flemish town. Nor were illustrated Bibles proscribed, nor lithographs of biblical stories. (For example, those of 39

Frans Menton, 1550–1615, in Haarlem, and of Claes Moeyaert, 1592/1655, in Amsterdam.) For the draughtsman Rembrandt the Bible with its stories, parables and miracles was an inexhaustible source of inspiration.

The Bible says (Luke 2, 21): "And on the eighth day the child was circumcised and he was called Jesus." Rembrandt drew the religious ceremony as if he were present at it. With a few strokes he indicated a spacious temple. The presence of two onlookers seemed important to him; he had probably seen them shortly before he drew the picture. He let the men react differently: the one with the high hat is sceptical, the other with the wide turban is naively amazed

Pl. 11   at what is going on. In Rembrandt's mind at least the two spectators were there in the first place. To relate their different attitudes to the Circumcision of Jesus was a later idea of Rembrandt's.

Pl. 12   Rembrandt often drew, etched and painted the parable of the Prodigal Son who already during his father's lifetime has received his inheritance and squandered it. Of the departure of the son the Bible says only (Luke 15, 13): "And not long afterwards the younger son gathered everything together and departed for a far land." Rembrandt filled out the situation in a dramatic and moral sense. According to his version the mother made a great occasion of the departure; she comes with a farewell drink in a tall cup to the son standing at the door. But he cannot get away quickly enough. He ignores the cup, grasps his mother's left hand with his own left hand in a hasty grip and swings himself on to his horse. The father looks on with disapproval and sorrow, as if turned to stone. A houseboy placed between the father and mother, by his expression and bearing, emphasises by contrast the visible emotion of the parents. Rembrandt had also thought of a servant for the young master: he, a figure in the background, holds the horse on a short rein. In the end Rembrandt decided not to include this figure, presumably because it weakened the impact of the son. After everything had been put down on paper Rembrandt accentuated parts of the drawing with a blunt instrument. He strengthened the figures of the two chief characters — the father and son, and underlined the figure of the father with thick strokes. On the left the dog has been added to round off the composition: the feeling of home is indicated by the tone wash on the open door.

Pl. 13   It is possible that the drawing with the tric-trac players belongs in imagination to the same circle of thought as the parable of the Prodigal Son. The player on the right has the costume, the one on the left the facial features of the son in the drawing of the "Departure." All three expressions in the drawing link themselves to portray evil deeds: the reckless gambler, the idle smoker, the drunken man with the grinning girl.

If here and there pictures are connected with the same theme, that does not imply that Rembrandt drew picture stories with one explaining and expanding the other. The "Tric-Trac Players" is in thought complete in itself. The subject matter of "Parting" is in no way bound up with the parable of the prodigal son, but it is a fundamental basic theme which he explored as a

40   complex of diverging thoughts and feelings.

Because of the method and manner in which Rembrandt expanded in his drawings episodes *Pl. 14* described in a few words in the Bible, it is not surprising that not all the sketches can be linked with definite passages. The dramatically composed group of the old man with two youthful figures is one such drawing: a bearded man in a high hat and dignified clothing, opposed by two youths in long, phantastic drapings. The old man is protesting and turns away with embarrassed gestures; one of the youths is replying with great anger, while the other alarms the old man with his stony composure.

So much the more meaningful is the drawing which was owned by Goethe, Lot and his *Pl. 16* daughters after the destruction of Sodom. The wine has not yet robbed the old man of all reflection, as his daughters with their determined looks and movements wish. If one notices a related manner between the daughters (button-eyed, and tight-lipped in the one, trapezoid nose and double receding chin in the other) and the two youths of the previous, unidentified scene, drawn presumably at the same time, then one is tempted to connect this other picture with the story of Lot. The often painted scene of Lot's encounter with the two angels whom he invites to stay overnight at his house, is certainly not depicted here. The old man is certainly not extending an invitation with *this* expression and *these* gestures, the two young men are *no* angels and are not declining an invitation. Rather Rembrandt could have thought of the Bible words describing how Lot refused to bring out his guests, the two angels. The womanly dress of the youths would then be meant as a reference to the sin of the Sodomites – homosexuality, which is still known as Sodomy.

Less generally understood were episodes in the history of the Roman Republic, which found favour as subjects for pictures with townsmen, and the myths and heroic sagas of ancient days. Achievements of the Roman republicans had gained a place in the thoughts of Dutch burghers since the end of the fifteenth century and comparisons were made with their own achievements, while later court art with the rise of absolutism sought to find similarities between the Greek and Roman world of the gods and the deeds and thoughts of kings, queens and their courts. Rembrandt was familiar with both groups of ideas. He did not take Ovid's gods seriously, as the Dresden "Ganymede" and the Prince Salmsche "Diana Bathing" show. The virtues of the Romans were, however, worth considering.

Manius Curius Dentatus in Warsaw belongs to these. With apparent cordiality costly pre- *Pl. 15* sents are being offered, and with great anger they are being refused. When drawing this picture Rembrandt had thought of the superficially related but circumstantially different scene which he etched in 1629, where Jacob is shown the bloodstained coat of Joseph (Bartsch 38). There it was the liar who brought the false report; it was the horror at the supposed death of the favourite son. In Curius Dentatus it is the seemingly sincere offering and the morally necessary refusal. Such themes, brought into the orbit of contemporary thought, were apposite to the young Dutch Republic and its presentation. Rembrandt's pupil, 41

Ferdinand Bol, made a note of this composition, and later — about 1662 — used it as the basis for his painting for the Amsterdam City Hall.

Pl. 18 With the "Flute Player" we return to Rembrandt's studio and to direct observation. The armchair with the curved legs had been part of the studio furnishings in Leiden. A pupil playing the flute in a pause from work and the boy standing on the left behind the table listening to him formed the basic situation. Rembrandt introduced, as separation and contrast, the pupil who is not listening but working, and then, to balance the composition, he indicated with a few lines the listener sitting on the edge of the table.

Although, until the early days of Rembrandt's Amsterdam period, only drawings of individual people and groups of people have been considered and illustrated, this is not by choice or accident. People alone and in company had so far entirely captivated Rembrandt's interest. In his thirtieth year for the first time — perhaps because he felt he owed it to his pupils — animals and landscapes came to the fore. Exotic animals, such as dromedaries, elephants and birds of paradise, that Rembrandt and his pupils "needed" for their compositions, were on show in *Pl. 20* menageries in Amsterdam, and he drew them most probably in company with his pupils. This is confirmed by a note written by a pupil on the drawing of the dromedary with its two eastern attendants.

Landscape at that time held no attraction for Rembrandt. He was a townsman who needed the bustle of the town around him as the source from which he could gain an understanding of men and their ways. Rural surroundings offered no equivalent — even in the country house on the outskirts of the town.

Pl. 19 The few landscapes of his thirties seem merely incidental. The beautiful drawing owned by Goethe (who with due respect had it stamped with only part of his name) is full of light and contrasting forms. The static house with the landing stage is offset by the living force of the up-thrusting trees; the brightness of the tree on the left is opposed to the deep shadows in the farmhouse on the right, and, reconciling these opposites, a duologue of light and shade plays in the trees on the far bank.

Pl. 22 & 23 The two splendid Budapest drawings tell us a great deal about Rembrandt's contemplation of nature. These drawings were made from almost the same viewpoint in the course of a few hours. A farmhouse, planned and built in a most complicated way, lies in bright sunlight. It is over-grown with a climbing shrub. Rembrandt leaves the outline of the building vague. What he pondered over and drew were static forms made unclear by the growing vine, vegetation softening the hard outlines of the shadows. Light heightened light and darkness deepened in the shade — that was what Rembrandt saw, considered and drew. A few hours later when the slanting shadows from the front part of the roof fell on the wall to the right, he made another drawing of the corner of the farm building seen from a short distance. Now the ancient vine dominates the picture, as it spreads unhindered on every side, having at last reached the roof by toilsome spirals. Seen from close up, it has subjugated the architecture. As always, the entrance to the house seems important to Rembrandt; he has employed the whole magic of his art to make the door and the gable appear as welcome as possible by shielding the entrance from the heat of the sun and from the rampant vegetation.

The founding of his own household after his marriage with Saskia in the year 1634 opened up a new world for Rembrandt – the world of women and children. Drawings made during the following years show clearly his enjoyment of domesticity, and make paintings like the large Dresden double portrait of himself with Saskia on his knee at a Zecherstück (a drinking bout with everyone paying for their own drinks) seem quite out of character. This painting, together with the Dresden "Ganymede" and the Frankfurt "Blinding of Samson" seem to suggest his intention to vie with the work of the baroque court painters and to out-trump them.

As far as he himself and his immediate environment are concerned, he remains the hyper- *Pls. 1* critical reasoner with the probing eye, as he had depicted himself in 1626/28 when he was a *& 24* young independent artist in Leiden. The richly toned, lucid brushwork of the portrait with the palette hanging near him on the wall belongs approximately to 1635. It is clear and decisive. There is no conflict between light and dark in the face; instead this face is illumined by the brightness of the surrounding space, which softens the shadows and emphasises the reflected light. Rembrandt must have attached great importance to the sensitive execution of this self-portrait for, with the greatest care, he went over the whole drawing with a wash.

He had come by chance on Saskia as she slept and made two drawings one after the other, *Pl. 26* noting how her features and limbs relaxed more and more as sleep deepened.

A sketch of Saskia sitting up in bed he later turned into a small picture by adding a few bold *Pl. 25* strokes.

Now the mother and child theme excited Rembrandt's imagination, as in the group of three *Pl. 27* – nurse, mother and baby. In 1635, 1638 and 1640 children were born to him, but they soon died. From almost the first days of their infancy Rembrandt followed them around with a quill-pen. In a beautiful group he sketched mother, baby and an "aunt," the baby apathetic – unconscious of the surroundings – the mother tense, the "aunt" curious.

Later there followed a child's first efforts to stand – supported by a nursemaid's arm, and now *Pl. 28* looking round to see what impression he is making on others. In a small boy being carried down *Pl. 29* some steps into the open air, Rembrandt saw above all else awakening self-will. It is clear from the drawing that he first drew loose, hasty strokes to capture the child's behaviour and expression in the mother's arms, and then carefully added the whole figure of the woman, and showed her climbing down out of the shadow into the light.

Now Rembrandt began to notice other people's children. What his own did not offer, he gathered in the streets and brought home as comparative experiences from his walks in the   43

Pl. 30 town. One of these is the obstinacy of the little child who is waging war with an old servant or grandmother, and now stubbornly stays behind, tyrannising the old woman with screams of *Pl. 31* fury. Then, too, Rembrandt saw the father who, with an anxious look, has embarked on the unusual task of feeding the baby. For his pains he earns first astonishment, then refusal and finally screaming protest, because the child misses his mother's presence. Rembrandt drew the consecutive phases of this little drama with growing understanding of the childish mind.

Pl. 32 As Rembrandt watched a small, self-willed imp who, still half-naked, had run out of the house and has now to be dragged back in the mother's firm grip, the artist built up what he saw into an imagined scene. As a dramatist he introduced the two mischievous little boys in the doorway who add to the child's burst of anger. He gave the mother support in the guise of a grandmother whose senseless admonition with the upraised finger makes more telling the resolute grip of the mother and her expression of mingled anger and concern.

Pl. 33 By what devious paths Rembrandt wandered from this rebellious struggling child to the boy Ganymede, beloved by the father of the gods, Zeus, we do not know. The same child is no longer in his mother's arms, but in the claws of the eagle whose shape Zeus has assumed, as he carries the king's son from earth up to the Olympic heights. The child's face is recognisibly the starting part of the drawing. Nevertheless, Rembrandt is already conscious of the new situation as a whole: he has changed the child's expression — instead of anger as in the first drawing, it is now one of fear. He has depicted the strength of the eagle rather than its form, to indicate the irresistible upward journey bearing the heavy weight of the child's body. With a whirr of excited lines he represents screams and clamour, with a faint wash he visibly separates eagle, child's body and the little shirt. Unfortunately a pedantic graphic "frame" cuts through the drawing above, below and on the left, and weakens the dynamic impact of the picture.

How Rembrandt came on the thought of enlarging the drawing into this composition is hard to understand. He disliked baroque painting with its predeliction for scandalous and brutal motifs. The most likely explanation is that he wanted to introduce beauty into the baroque and to carry it out with consummate artistry.

Pl. 35 With the child on the leading rein, we return to the domestic scene. Fitted out with the comic and practical Dutch "fall-hat" — a sort of padded "helmet" for protection in possible tumbles — the child embarks on his first steps. Rembrandt has noted that the reins are not held horizontally as they are when "playing horses," but must be kept at a sharp angle from above. By the side of the drawing Rembrandt has hastily sketched a small tragedy which the maid has not yet noticed: the hat has slipped forward over the child's eyes; he can see nothing and his cry of protest is just making itself heard.

Pl. 34 Once again Rembrandt has built up the study of a child into a compositional picture. He had noticed how terrified a small child was when a dog ran up to him in the street. The animal's

44 friendliness was frightening because the soft snout was just on a level with the child's face. In

Rembrandt's drawing the mother behaves sensibly. She has put down her shopping basket and with both arms draws the child to her to comfort him. She hides her anxiety beneath apparent calm. Rembrandt quickly indicates the significance of the setting: only in a street would the unexpected encounter with a strange dog be possible. Inside the house is safety, and from there one can survey street scenes coolly and with detachment. In the composition the figure at the window was introduced to emphasise by contrast the deep affection and kindliness of the mother.

Reference has already been made to the concept of Inside and Outside. For Rembrandt, to whom Light and Darkness were realities, this borderline between light and dark was both psychologically and physiologically a source of continuous meditation. One is tempted to relate more closely the two drawings which show door scenes from inside and out. From the interior of the house the eye is blinded by the daylight. One does not know what is happening outside and what has caught the attention of the three women. Here again, as can be seen in the alteration to the head of the standing woman, Rembrandt first drew a hasty sketch of what he saw and then made a compositional drawing. The three women are placed in different relationships to the light and therefore do not correspond with true optical conditions. The seated figure seen from behind belongs to the house, only the narrow strip of light on her head connects her with the street. The figure of the woman on the right is divided, with the sunlit lower half of the door light breaks into the darkness which surrounds her, but her body darkness obstructs the light. The woman on the threshold is completely outside, and so is entirely in the light, although her back must throw a body shadow. The changes that Rembrandt made in the drawing showed still more clearly the parallel between light-dark and outside-inside. A light standing figure outside was washed out: it had nothing more to add to the significance of the woman on the threshold. The head of the standing woman had to be so altered that it belonged, with its unusual transparency, both to the light and to the darkness.

In the house is safety; outside the door lies the uncertain realm of the homeless and the hounded. They come begging with their collecting box and drum: even as children they run about the streets.

Rembrandt saw very clearly that street children and house children are very different. The house children take care not to venture beyond the safety of the door. But the imprudent movements of the smallest child are straining the arms of the nursemaid. Rembrandt has rounded out this drawing, and has put a wash over the grown-ups, the door and the entrance, to lessen their importance in the picture. The main theme was intended to be the street children and the house children.

Saskia gave birth to four children, of whom three died very young. Judging by the number of drawings that Rembrandt made of Saskia during her confinements or when she was ill in bed, one must suppose that he often lingered near at hand with pen and paper. Saskia and her

Pl. 41

Pl. 40

45

Pl. 42 attendant were no doubt so accustomed to the silent draughtsman that the maid could chatter unrestrainedly while Saskia listened, weak and morbidly excited.

With the mother-and-child theme in mind, one can clearly recognize the development of "truth" in the pictures. In "Simeon in the Temple" (Hamburg, Kunsthalle), painted in about 1628, the attitude of the child with its little arm upraised beside the unsupported head is quite impossible. Then, too, when in 1630 he painted Mary feeding the Christ Child on the flight to Egypt Rembrandt still knew very little about mothers and children. But in 1635/36 among the people listening to the preaching of John the Baptist (Berlin-Dahlem) in the groups of mothers and children we can see his newly gained knowledge clearly shown in the childish bodies.

Pl. 45 When Rembrandt was in his thirties the publication of a engraving of Leonardo da Vinci's "Last Supper" gave rise to a good deal of discussion. More than a hundred years earlier the Italian master had demonstrated in this work his belief that there was a connection between men's words and their physical characteristics. Rembrandt's first drawing on this subject (which was earlier preserved in Dresden) followed the Leonardo print fairly closely. Rembrandt retained the four groups of three disciples with which Leonardo refuted the medieval teaching of the four temperaments. He emphasised the facial expressions, weakened the "speech" of the hands. Leonardo's disciples are meant to show twelve different ways in which men of distinctive types might react to the accusation "One of you will betray me." Their response would, according to Leonardo's interpretation, be determined by their physical characteristics. This very definite standpoint of Leonardo's then passed into the teaching of all sixteenth century western art. In his rendering of the Last Supper Rembrandt overruled this current scholastic teaching: he no longer made words conform to types, but made them dependant on bodily deportment, facial expression and the reaction' of other people. The profit he gained from his study of the composition of the Last Supper showed less in his drawings than in his large paintings, because his drawings were almost always concerned with individual people and their relation to one another. There are few drawings in which he has made division into groups or architectural construction the primary subject of his consideration.

Pl. 44 The Dresden "Ecce Homo" drawing, which has already been referred to in our consideration of Rembrandt's musings in chalk, can serve again here as an example of a "classic" composition based on a drawing reminiscent of Leonardo. The original idea of the path to the execution, with the criminal, the executioner and the comforter, has its parallel in a drawing in which *Pl. 43* Rembrandt follows the course of the execution, and depicts the scene of the beheading and finally the headless body. The Dresden drawing in its last phase has become the great composition "Ecce Homo", by Rembrandt's decision to reverse its implication and to place the people from the back of the drawing in the forefront of the picture. Unfortunately a large piece 46 is missing from the sheet – torn out of the left-hand side.

Into the years 1636 to 1638 falls, too, a group of drawings inspired by processions and exhibi- *Pls. 46*
tions. They are careful works which seem to suggest that they have been made for reference. *47*
The back view of a woman in rich costume suggests a play. The two theatrical villains would *48*
have belonged to a troupe of itinerant actors; and the negro drummers on mules, with the cere-
monial umbrella-bearer in the rear might have formed part of a pageant acclaiming the newly
established South African Cape Colony, or in some way relating to the world-wide expansion
of Holland's sphere of influence.

The scene in the market place where a "Quack" is boosting his wares was already "set" so *Pl. 49*
completely that Rembrandt only needing a passing glance to choose it for a future composition.
He made several sketches of the scene one after the other, and while doing so distributed the
interest in various ways. In the accompanying illustration the deeply sceptical onlookers have
captured his attention; the train of thought they evoked ends in the entirely disinterested figure
in the left foreground.

Rembrandt no doubt adapted impressions gained at annual fairs or in theatres to the shepherd *Pl. 50*
playing the flute with the two women listening to him. Rembrandt has caught the shepherd
just at the moment when, with blown-out cheeks and with hands wrongly placed, he is playing
a wooden flute. He builds up a comic group with the shepherdess looking as though she could
scarcely believe her ears. Rembrandt developed it into a landscape in a second phase with a
seated figure seen from the back, with sheep and a fold. As in "Ecce Homo" (Pl. 44) the finished
picture no longer corresponds with the first conception; the farcical group has been placed in a
serious setting.

At the time of his marriage to Saskia – that is also at the time of his greatest fame as painter
and artist in Holland – the Stadholder Frederick Henry of Nassau commissioned a number
of paintings of scenes from the life of Christ. This provided Rembrandt with an opportunity to
clarify the old theme of religious art: Angel and Man. In his paintings light and colour serve to
manifest the contact between heavenly beings and earthly creatures. In the drawings, however,
the problem was how to differentiate angels and mortals by their bearing. Rembrandt's angels
are consolers, helpers and advisers of men: he never drew revengeful or punitive angels. It
corresponds with the ethical character of his work in general that he regarded angels as the
embodiment of good and fruitful ideas, and sought to make them so understood by others.
He has brought these encounters to high drama when by chance an angel whom men had
accepted as one of themselves has suddenly revealed his heavenly nature.

"Manoah's Offering" unforgettably represented in the great Dresden painting, is one solution
to this problem, with the contrasting attitudes of the believing woman and the sceptical man.
Rembrandt gave another interpretation in the Paris painting, where an angel – unsuspected by
the families of the old and the young Tobias – after a long sojourn as a mortal among mortals,
suddenly revealed his true nature and, flying, disappeared.

Pl. 51   A drawing from about 1639 shows Rembrandt occupied with both interpretations at the same time. Above the smoke wreaths from a sacrificial fire (belonging to the Manoah story) an angel rises diagonally heavenwards: it is less his wings than his transfigured body encircled with spiral lines that is dynamic. The reaction of the two people to the ascension of the angel, as Rembrandt has depicted it, does not fit into the Manoah situation. The woman should not show such great surprise, and the man would surely have been aware only of the sacrificial fire. As in the Execution and Ecce Homo drawings, Rembrandt has not illustrated but has interpreted the Bible, His subject here was solely the speedy recognition of the two people and the different effects it had on the man and the woman.

Pl. 52   The encounter between the angel and Hagar in the wilderness is quite different. Abraham had turned Hagar out of his house with their son, at the request of Sarah, his lawful wife, who in her old age had experienced the joys of motherhood. Hagar and her child lost their way in the wilderness and were in danger of dying from thirst. Then an angel came to her, reawakened her mother-love and her will to live, and showed her the way to the saving well. According to the Bible story Hagar had left her son because she could not bear to see his suffering. The angel's rebuke is gentle: with a look in which incredulity and hope are mingled, Hagar turns towards the apparition without awe or fear.

So Rembrandt had learned to understand and depict supernatural visions as the personification of a man's inner voice, which for the time being they must resemble as closely as possible.

Earlier, about 1633/34, when he had attempted to depict the story of Balaam and his ass (Paris, Musée Cognacy-Jay, 1626) he avoided the angel motif in paintings, drawings and etchings. But after meditating, in thought and line, on the higher beings of biblical teaching, they entered into his works as a matter of course.

Another facet of his artistic production in his late thirties was the baroque treatment of biblical stories. Originally the baroque school of painting (and also of sculpture and architecture) produced thoughtful work on a high moral level, but, later, mystic devotion was crowded out by sensuality. "Susannah and the Elders," "Joseph and Potiphar's Wife," "Delilah's Betrayal *Pl. 53* of Samson," belong to Rembrandt baroque. Susannah and Joseph are falsely accused; Samson is a sacrifice to corruption and betrayal. With the Susannah theme Rembrandt is still in the realm of moral teaching: a beautiful woman taken by surprise must ward off the importunities of two lustful old men. In 1641 Rembrandt had first tried to portray Susannah alone, as she shrank back alarmed by suspicious rustlings in the thick bushes. But then he had brought one of the old men close behind her, grasping her with his hand, and so Susannah's original attitude and expression were no longer suited to the situation.

Pl. 54   Rembrandt twice painted Delilah's calumny of Samson. In 1636 he used all the richness of the   Flemish baroque style, but in a manner totally unlike the beautifully composed "Sufferings of the

Martyrs" of the school of painting. In his drawing, made years later, he seems to question whether such a betrayal can be so simply accomplished. Now Delilah looks thoughtfully at the sleeping man and plays idly with the long hair to which Samson owes his unconquerable strength. Uncertainly, Delilah sways between truth and falsehood, while Samson's demon waits impatiently for her sign. In this way the story takes on a psychological depth of meaning, which marks Rembrandt's development during the first decade of his Amsterdam period.

In the years following Saskia's death, around 1641/43, Rembrandt made an intensive study of the environs of Amsterdam. This landscape offered nothing that could be called "comforting." Everywhere cultivated land told of the industry, orderliness and endurance of the Dutch people. The unique charm of the interminable horizontals of canals and dykes, the well-kept farmstead, windmill, or group of trees in the wide plain was first discovered by Rembrandt's generation; Rembrandt himself first recognised it less as a painter, more as an etcher and draughtsman.

The great master of the lowland scene was Hercules Seghers, who died about 1638/40. He was some twenty years older than Rembrandt, who held him in great esteem and in 1657 owned eight of his paintings. Von Seghers, personally or through his works, seems to have been the first to rouse Rembrandt to a more than casual duologue with the landscape. From the earliest *Pls. 56* of these drawings one can tell that the dramatist and developing psychologist Rembrandt did not *57* immediately find himself at home in this seemingly prosaic environment. In all three sketches *58* the middle distance and background were divided by tone from one another: there was no foreground, as was indeed a fact when the drawing was made from a dyke or canal bank. Nevertheless, this irritated Rembrandt, and so all three sketches were altered, probably after he had returned to his studio, by the insertion of heavy strokes indicating the nearer bank, and suggestions of sluices or bridges and people were introduced.

First steps into the wide landscape were tentative. As a townsman Rembrandt still turned to the near view, to which he was accustomed even out of doors. The changing moods of the *Pl. 61* weather came to meet the dramatist, as he built up a farmstead from areas of light and shade in the glow of the setting sun after a storm.

It was not long, however, before Rembrandt was thoroughly familiar with all the charac- *Pl. 60* teristic elements of the surroundings of Amsterdam. In a drawing such as the view of the town with the windmill and the church he developed a nature study into a compositional picture which might almost serve as model for a Dutch town view. The little chalk drawing with the overhanging bush by the canal shows the delicate charm of the landscape. The diagonal view, *Pl. 59* which Rembrandt used here for the first time, is particularly suited to give spatial depth to the picture. The reflections in the water, the dimming of the forms as they recede into the distance as far as the misty silhouette of the windmill present without dramatic light effects the enduring character and the fleeting moods of the prospect. Rembrandt enclosed the small sketch, so 49 making a picture from it, with the tree trunk on the left, the roofed posts on the right, and the boards of the landing stage below – these last were superimposed on the reflections in the water that he had drawn previously. With many alterations Rembrandt used this scene for an etching in 1645 (Bartsch 231). It is strange to see how his mind was occupied with biblical rather than Dutch themes while he studied the landscape. Without regard to the factual possi-

Pl. 62 bilities of the landscape picture, he experimented with natural and man-made forms and contrived glimpses into strange fields.

Pl. 65 In the years around and after Saskia's death Rembrandt's draughtsmanship was calmer, but it was filled with greater inner tension. Sketches of totally unrelated subjects on one sheet of paper seem typical of his output at this time. He had noticed three Orientals in an Amsterdam street being harangued by a Dutchman with an excited expression and gesticulations. If Rembrandt had seen a man so agitated a few years earlier he would have considered him the most important figure in the group and would have made him the central point of interest in the picture. Now this figure is almost hidden by the Orientals, whose composure clearly shows that they cannot understand the torrent of words pouring from the Dutchman. There is no connection between this group and the beggar drawn (apparently earlier) left and right of the group. In the sketch on the left the old man goes apathetically on his way. But in the sketch on the right Rembrandt has anticipated Picasso by drawing two expressions, one following closely on the other: the keen glance when the beggar notices someone approaching him who is likely to be "profitable," then, in a second pair of eyes sketched above the first, the humble look which accompanies the begging gesture.

We have already seen how a train of thought leads to a sudden transition in the drawings, so we dare also speak of the train of observation which now becomes apparent, and conclude from these sketches that Rembrandt intended in these middle years of his life to make the most fleeting or hidden emotion the cardinal point of his creative work. At this particular time he developed his experiments with chiaroscuro to make statements about the appearance and feelings of the people he drew. At first the enrichment of the light-dark scale served as foundation. He placed extremes of brilliance and darkness close together and afterwards worked outwards from them.

Pl. 63
Pls. 71
& 70
Pl. 69

Pl. 71 In the "Eve of the Epiphany" it is the figure seen from behind with the shining star; in the "Good Samaritan" the horse in front of the torch; in the Mount of Olives scene Jesus in front of the overhanging rock; and in the "Carpenter's Family," the craftsman in front of the window, where the poles of light and darkness meet. The arrival of the Good Samaritan at the inn by night is a story unmistakably constructed around light. A bright torch illuminates the group with the wounded man, giving reality and meaning to the actions of the people concerned. The innkeeper on the stairs appears undecided in the light of the flickering candle in his hands. The

planes of light are calmer where a lamp on the wall shines on the figure of the sleeping stable-boy near the horse. Finally the sharply defined frames of the windows with the silhouettes of the curious spectators symbolise the security of the people within the house.

The theme of the Good Samaritan, which Rembrandt often drew and still more often painted and etched, has sometimes been linked with Rembrandt's life, as have also the "Holy Family" (1645) in Leningrad, and the "Woodcutter's Family" (1646) in Cassel; people have imagined that they could see in them an expression of unfulfilled wishes. Naturally they have a general connection with his own family life, but we do not think they in any way reflect his own feelings. It is precisely those subjects which Rembrandt returned to again and again – the good Samaritan, the prodigal son, the Tobias story – that have no parallel in Rembrandt's life. Rembrandt worked into these parables and stories the same significance that they had in the Bible – moral teaching for the people of his day. These subjects, in contrast to, say, Susannah at the bath, Judith and Holofernes, were seldom included in baroque art, and Rembrandt could therefore rely only their content to attract the particular interest which he hoped would serve to bring home the moral teaching.

But Rembrandt is always the artist, and so is always striving to perfect the ways and means by which he can present his ideas in picture form. How does light influence the emotions? How can a frame of mind be interpreted in light-dark? – Those were problems on which the artist Rembrandt worked. There are two drawings of a family in a room, which are closely connected one with the other, and which, considered side by side, seem to be experimental. One is of a large, high room flooded with light; the other is gloomy, but only because Rembrandt has placed himself in a different position and is working in the light instead of in the shadow. Now the window is in the middle of the picture; the bed and the armchair have been moved from the left of the group of women to their right. So the two closely related drawings make it quite clear that the same room with the same people can appear to be absolutely different, and can be so depicted, according to whether the artist views it from out of the shadows, looking into the room bathed in light, or from the exactly opposite end, where, dazzled by the brilliance, he sees the boundaries of light and darkness blurred, and his ability to distinguish objects in the zone of darkness is diminished.

Pls. 68 & 69

Harmony and restful comfort are inherent in both drawings. In the picture where the room is bathed in light, Rembrandt has linked the man working at the bench with the women by light and shade over a wide distance. In the dark picture one sees with astonishment that, in spite of the closer spatial connection between the people, the man remains isolated, because the darkness is quiescent and affords no connection.

How Rembrandt "speaks" in light and shade can also be seen in a large drawing made during these same years 1642/44. The Abraham-Sarah-Hagar conflict was a theme that renaissance and baroque artists had rarely painted, but Rembrandt strove to understand its meaning. He sketched a gloomy entrance to the house from which Sarah peered jealously at Abraham as he parted

Pl. 66

51

with a fatherly blessing and comforting words from his son Ismael and Hagar, his second "wife." As Rembrandt stuck a piece of paper over the figure of Abraham and then made another drawing over it, it can be assumed that nothing is left in the picture which does not express his final intention. Abraham's turban, his forehead and eyes are intentionally dark in tone, and so he is brought into relation with Sarah over the light-enveloped figure of Hagar. Light and dark become the symbols of the emotions of the people in this picture-story.

Pl. 67   In another sketch of the same date Rembrandt has pondered on the situation in the house after Hagar has been sent away from it. While Hagar and Ismael are in the wilderness at the point of starvation (Pl. 52) Abraham sits grimly by the fire, with Hagar's empty chair in front of him, reading to Sarah. She sits beside him with a submissive air, now that she has got her own way. To the right of the room stands the cradle of the son Isaac, whose miraculous birth has given the old woman her power over Abraham. Dreaming, as it were, Rembrandt transforms the theme again; the old man sits, now blind, by the fire; his wife works near him at the spinning wheel: Tobias and his industrious wife, who wait expectantly for the return of their son. (Painting, 1659. In private possession, Rotterdam.)

Reference has already been made to Rembrandt's work on the theme "Angel and Man." His occupation with the Tobias story in his forties centres again on this problem in art. Rembrandt's angels have their wings for the enlightenment of the spectator of the picture, but not for the people in the picture. (Rembrandt has indeed introduced completely undogmatic bearded and bald-headed angels, thus making it quite clear that their wings are to serve only as a definite, clarifying symbol for the spectator: Etching, Bartsch 29). In the picture angels must show themselves superior to human beings by their comportment, expression and deeds, but they must not reveal their higher nature. When, however, the subject demands recognition of their divinity, then streams of light — not wings — serve for recognition.

Pl. 72   We see the young Tobias recoiling from the great fish which swims towards him as he washes in the Tigris. The angel stands calmly by, and says that the fish must be caught. Years later
Pl. 74   Rembrandt drew the next stage of the encounter. Tobias has recovered from his first shock, the angel still insists on action, but Tobias has to fight his fear that the great fish will attack him.
Pl. 73   But then the deed is done. Tobias looks questioningly towards the friend, towards the angel, only to learn that he must now disembowel the dead fish. At each stage the angel is only a helpful friend to Tobias. In these sketches it can clearly be seen how Rembrandt, after he has considered the subject from all aspects, has broadened the landscape and used it, too, to emphasise the spiritual teaching. A fleeting comparison of the turbulent scenery at the first sight of the fish (Pl. 72) with the idyllic countryside surrounding Tobias and the dead fish, makes this obvious.

At the same time the Tobias drawings present a dialogue. Separation between men was from
52   the beginning of his thirties a cardinal theme of Rembrandt's. In the beginning he had relied on

pathetic looks and emphatic facial expression to convey speech and hearing. Now he tried with fewer lines and sparser tones to convey deeper truths.

A drawing with rough blobs left standing and with finger smudges is nevertheless a miracle *Pl. 75* of psychological understanding. Again the scene is taken from the Tobias story. The suddenly blinded old Tobias accuses his diligent wife of having may be stolen a goat, which has in fact been given to her. Never before had the situation been so vividly presented. Rembrandt makes the woman react to the morbid mistrust not with tearful or pathetic complaint, but with counter-attack and a threat to leave the ingrate in the lurch. In spite of all the accidental blots and thickening of the tones, every stroke is full of meaning; the spots on the stool could stay, as also the finger smears between its legs, because they only bound old Tobias, as a blind man, more firmly to the seat.

The same theme was one of the first painted by Rembrandt as the young master (1926. Now in Paris, the Bentinck-Thyssen collection). The Book of Tobias, from which Rembrandt never freed himself throughout his life, was apparently so arresting, not because simple men of the Old Testament in their belief, joy, sorrow, fear, well-being or sin were described there, but because the doubting, the irresolute, and those acting under compulsion against commonsense were exactly like people of his own time within their own civilisation which had already grown highly complicated. The Tobias story had never been a subject for fine art until Rembrandt so used it.

The dualogue as Rembrandt drew it now included the wordless dialogue and dumb perception.

The return of the prodigal son to the father, which he drew for the first time in 1645, belongs *Pl. 76* here. Without a word being said, the son kneels on the threshold of the paternal home. Rembrandt has made clear in his attitude an awareness of his sin and a plea for forgiveness, just as he makes clear in the father's bearing a matter-of-course forgiveness, sympathy and concern. A young boy with an indescribable look of precocious scepticism, participation and curiosity, is an objective witness of the proceedings, as is so often the case with Rembrandt. He reflects the casual interest of the uninvolved and emphasises by antithesis, the voice of humanity, which can be perceived in the central characters.

A wordless but complete understanding exists between the working couple in the room that *Pl. 77* in its inspiration reminds one of a "Holy Family." A similar silent unanimity of thought and *Pl. 90* deed prevails in the drawing of the blind beggar, his boy and the householder. Rembrandt has adapted it, too, in the Paris "Bathsheba," which he painted in 1654.

In a drawing made in his forties we see him on the way to perfecting this idea. According to Ovid's "Metamorphoses," a book much favoured in high society at the time, the god Vertumnus has been changed into an old woman and endeavours in this guise to convince Pomona of the charms of Vertumnis, that is, of himself. Rembrandt drew the old woman with youthful, lustfully shining eyes, ready to spring. But Pomona is entirely shut up within herself and weighs 53 up in her mind the results of acceptance or refusal. — Certainly an easier choice to make than that which confronted Rembrandt's Bathsheba of 1654.

Pl. 95 How far Rembrandt developed his potentialities is shown on a sheet with a man dictating to a secretary. It is a fully worked out, rounded off composition, which does not record a momentary impression but follows through an idea. If it is concerned with a biblical subject, then it is certainly not the parable of the unjust steward; for then Rembrandt would indeed be a bungler in characterisation. Obviously a highly energetic letter is being dictated. But the master is not speaking; he has his partner before him in his thoughts, bores through him with his looks and flings his accusations in his face. Apart from the master's sub-conscious phantasy, on the conscious level he pours scorn on his secretary, who clearly shows how little all this disturbs him, and only exerts himself to make sure that he does not mishear or omit a single word. No precedent can be found even in Rembrandt's own work for the way in which the brushstrokes in the body and legs of the master and in the tablecloth help to stress the anger of the man, while on the other side of the table the calm horizontals and verticals emphasise the indifference of the secretary. There was no comparable scene in the whole of western art before that time.

Pl. 80 The temptation of Jesus by Satan is reminiscent of "Vertumnus and Pomona" (Pl. 79). Rembrandt neither wished to nor could he present a devil or any evil spirits, although the Dutch had a rich tradition of both in Hieronymous Bosch and Breughel the Elder. Rembrandt tried to represent Satan by the circuitous means of a skeleton; the few other material symbols for devils in his drawings depend on antique fauns or bats. This shows that Rembrandt did not "invent"; the inspiration for his work came from the visible world. The psychological content of his work certainly often anticipates mental concepts and emotions of men of later generations, for example in Goethe's time. The actual model for this Satan was a skeleton used for instruction in the anatomical theatre of Amsterdam University. The skeletons were in fact mounted in universities in the pose of equestrian statues. Rembrandt studied this objectively when he drew *Pl. 81* the "Triumph of Death," and even included the supporting iron which carried the whole structure and was absolutely necessary to ensure the majestically rigid attitude of the skeleton rider.

In these years of his forties Rembrandt covered the widest field of subjects. To scenes of contemporary life, to the Old and New Testaments and the Apocrypha, he added classical mythology, Homeric verse, heroic sagas and romance to the scope of his work. During his first years in Amsterdam he had adopted the baroque style in form and composition, particularly as an etcher and painter, but he had never chosen a typically baroque subject. Now such themes occur more often in his work, but he develops them in his own individual way with an inner non-baroque tension gained from his study of thought and emotions. He did not, however, paint such subjects; he only drew them. He wanted to discover for himself what he might
54 achieve by this means.

To this experimental period belongs the idyll of the flute-playing shepherd and the singing *Pls. 82 & 83* "gardener" – that is Mercury and Argus – a myth much altered in the drawing. Cunningly Mercury lulls to sleep the hundred-eyed Argus whom Jupiter has told to keep watch over Io, his beloved, now transformed into a heifer. With a sharp eye on Argus, Mercury draws from its scabbard the sword that until now has been carefully hidden, so that he may kill the sentinel.

It is characteristic of Rembrandt's association with the thought-world of court baroque that he avoided such popular themes as Leda and the Swan, Luna and Endymion, Amor and Psyche, Cimon and Pero, and the naked Lucretia, because they were for the most part only of erotic but not of psychological interest.

Rembrandt obviously took great pains with the drawing which shows the daughters of Cecrops – in defiance of the prohibition of the goddess Athene – opening a basket and now *Pl. 84* seeing Erichthonius with his snake-like body. No one had painted this subject before Rembrandt. Its attraction for him would have been to show the different effects of this sudden horror on the women and to try to discover whether the overthrow of reason by madness could be conveyed through the medium of art. The many differences – in the attitude of the curious Aglauros on the left, who had opened the basket, in the movements of the two maids, in the faces, in the dog that had been added to the scene, show how he had grappled with the unpictorial theme.

Earlier Rembrandt had etched and drawn the dramatic scene of Jacob's sons showing their *Pl. 89* father the blood-stained coat of his favourite child Joseph, and deceiving him with the lie that Joseph was dead. Now Rembrandt chose form the same story – of Joseph – on which he always worked with pleasure, the scene where the sons have returned from Egypt. Here the talk is of the wonderful nobleman who has requested them to come back to Egypt, bringing with them their youngest brother, Benjamin. Again Rembrandt draws a dialogue, this time with very significant listeners. One of the brothers reports what all the others know except the old father Jacob and his favourite Benjamin. Calmly they listen, seeing again in memory the strange scenes which their brother is describing to their doubting father. The Bible text is by no means deficient in words at this point; Rembrandt knew it well and made the probing questions interjected by Jacob as clear as the embarassed cicumstantial answers of the son. The concise gestures – for instance, the expectant right hand of the father, the disconcerted left hand of the storyteller – have in their precision complete Bible sentences as content. With the cup that Benjamin holds ready for his father, Rembrandt hints at the later episode in which a cup in Benjamin's sack will play an apparently ominous role.

While Rembrandt at this time rejected – so far as drawing was concerned – themes that could *Pl. 88* only be interpreted in baroque style or from a catholic viewpoint, he did not reject miracles. He drew the contest between the God-fearing Elijah and the priests of the gods of Baal. What he produced is in the first place a magnificently bold composition in which he linked the feeling of spacial depth by cubes in the foreground and below to the background and on high. Then he staged the "miracle" in the picture exactly where it might be expected to occur at a first glance. The style is anti-baroque. He says what is most important quite plainly instead of in the baroque manner of concealment to flatter the "clever" and "shrewd" spectator. Only then, as it were in subsidiary positions does he comment on the servants of the gods and their unsuccessful strivings on behalf of the powerless Baal. The darkness of ignorance is symbolised by the image of Baal on the altar, engulfing the sacrificial beast and the heathen priests, while Elijah and his altar stand in the midst of a heaven sent miracle. Combined with the monumental silhouette of Elijah and the confused outline of the groups of priests is the grandeur of the plan and the depth of the statement, which is paralleled in Shakespeare's Brutus-Antony scene in "Julius Caesar", but is unequalled in pictorial art.

Pl. 92   Rembrandt retained this very direct form of statement when he recorded in a number of drawings his train of thought on the parable of the workers in the vineyard. His aim was to analyse the different reactions of the labourers in face of the seemingly peculiar justice of the owner of the vineyard when he paid the hired men. In the first drawing the ideas for a large composition are reminiscent of "Elijah" and similar works. The thoughts of the workers are less precise. The last of them looks like a meek recipient of alms.

Pl. 93   In the other picture the dispute between justice and injustice is fully developed. One worker holds his wage hesitantly in his hand and obviously does not in the least understand the argument of the vineyard owner. The other shows very definitely that he considers the higher justice of the owner sheer nonsense. The group of four having considered the matter accept the scale with typical indifference, indecision, resignation, appeasement.

Pl. 94   In a later painting Rembrandt's ideas on the parable of the labourers in the vineyard seem to have fused with those of the angry man dictating a letter (Pl. 95), and have resulted in the picture of the "Hidden Talent" based on the parable of unused ability. Linked with the sentence "To whomsoever hath, to him shall be given," this parable of the unfaithful servant who did not seek to gain a hundred per cent interest on his master's capital would be appreciated by Dutch business men. We are of the opinion that Rembrandt's sympathy would be with the servant while he drew, because he himself was held to be "unfaithful" in monetary matters by his wife's relatives.

    A number of landscape drawings are grouped around the impressions of a short journey — yet the longest Rembrandt is known to have made — towards the end of his forties. The stay in England, which some people have thought could be assumed because a few views of English towns were found among his papers, has been proved by research to be a myth. Rembrandt copied the views of London and Windsor, dated 1640, from pictures. The exhibitions in Rotterdam and Amsterdam in 1956, where these drawings were included, showed how remarkable they are.

The journey in 1646/47 took Rembrandt to Rhenen and Arnhem, some 56 miles south-east *Pl. 96* of Amsterdam. In Rhenen he was fascinated by the town fortifications, which exceeded in strength any he had so far seen. His most beautiful architectural drawings were made here. The malerisch (painterly) property of the old walls and the play of light and shadow in the deep double doors had never before been so faithfully recorded, although hundreds of painters and draughtsmen had made studies of buildings in Rome, and Holland possessed "architectural specialists" among its artists.

The drawing of a coach, which comes close to the artistic achievement of the views of Rhenen, *Pl. 97* proves – if that were necessary – that Rembrandt also possessed technical knowledge. The vehicle, a travelling coach with suspended coupé, may have intrigued him because in Amsterdam and its environs canal boats and pleasure yachts were more usual than coaches.

From 1650 to 1655 Rembrandt again took to the roads in the immediate neighbourhood of *Pls. 98 99 103* Amsterdam, as in earlier years, with his drawing pad, a lonely wanderer in the winter on the deserted dykes bordering the frozen canals. He captured the typical Dutch form of small settlement in ever new variations: the sheets of water, the dyke that kept the water under control, the village almost hidden behind the dyke, distinguishable by its church, or the farmstead near a large clump of trees.

His achievement with the landscape was in this period richer, because he was out in all seasons of the year, not only in summer. Several times he sought the same view in summer and winter. In the clear summer air he saw the firm outline of the houses, haystacks and trees, with the contrasts between the static surfaces of house and roof and the constantly changing play of light in the foliage. But in the winter the contours were blurred with mist, the trees and buildings in the diffused light were without plastic strength, but from the point of view of art they were enchanting, with most delicate differences in tone values (Pls. 100 and 101 of the same farmstead). For these drawings from nature, whose locality Fritz Lugt, with great penetration, has fixed in the near vicinity of Amsterdam, Rembrandt used very modest technical apparatus which he carried with him. It is a tribute to the eminent skill with which these sketches were made, that their striking effect has been accomplished with such simple means. The tree-lined *Pl. 106* dyke which dams the water on the right and separates it from the low lying field on the left is drawn with a coarse, cleft instrument, perhaps with a reed just plucked and trimmed. The shadows and washes are smeared with the finger. Rather more thinning of his drawing medium gave lighter colour tones; where, however, stronger lines are intended to show through, then the "dry brush" came into use, yielding thickish colour that flowed disconnectedly.

The full richness of the thatched cottage with the tall bushes by the canal, which he drew *Pl. 107* several times, was produced with a stumpy piece of wood that deposited only little daubs of colour. With a dampened finger Rembrandt softened these and smeared them to a tint. The piece of wood was used almost dry to sketch in the path, to carry out the artist's intention of accentuating the difference between the well-kept path and the unruly wildness of the vegetation.

On other wanderings he seems to have carried a small assortment of brushes, with which he drew pictures of striking originality and great charm. On broad toned planes he dotted about *Pl. 116* various forms — ships at anchor in a wide inlet, a mill, and groups of houses on the Amstel *Pl. 115* dyke — which remind one of Chinese drawings, but which are perhaps most nearly related to Dutch tile painting. In the little mill on the Amstel dam he played off the calm horizontals of the dyke, the surface of the water and the line of the bank against the varied shapes of buildings, and introduced a scarcely perceptible movement into the picture by means of the ship and its sail and masthead. He conveyed the breadth of water and sky, with the inlet of the sea behind the disturbing stockade in a break of the dyke, and inset the ship with a few brushwork dots — in such ways he made far-reaching statements with the simplest means and showed ultimate wisdom in the art of drawing.

Just as a short sentence in a biblical parable led Rembrandt on to further thought and then to working out the thought in drawing, so he often drew on his imagination when *Pl. 113* sketching landscapes, and this resulted in scenic compositions. By so doing he did not introduce mere stage properties. For instance, the large group of trees drawn perhaps on his journey to Rhenen and Arnhem was the starting point for the pictorial composition of the *Pl. 112* rider and his servant. The main line of the tree sketch is curved and imaginative; with the introduction of the dead tree on the right, it has become a scholastic composition. Then the trend of thought becomes clear. Rembrandt discarded the first conception of the servant: he brought him up closer to the rider and animated him, so that now his haste and the horseman's dilatoriness are contrasted. The corpse on the gallows as a warning, and the church tower as the knight's destination were further developments in the story.

Pl. 111   The drawing of the village street with the cows shows even more clearly how Rembrandt's imagination was aroused by a country scene. First he drew the group of cows, then the street with the trees and the church, the houses to left and right. Then playfully he introduced the horseman with the two dogs, and so forced on himself the necessity of filling out the left side of the picture, where the peasant now comes to the door of his house in greeting. So Rembrandt often indulged in a veritable art-play in which things could go awry just as with a story-teller, so that the initial situation no longer agreed with the outcome. In the sketch before us the group of ruminating cows appears most improbable now that it is surrounded by the village street, the rider, the hunting dogs and the peasant.

Pl. 110   In the splendid drawing of the resting reapers the group of people on the edge of the cornfield is of the first importance; the nearby mill and the distant un-Dutch hill were added, and finally *Pl. 109* the tree trunk was inserted on the left. In the sketch with the drawbridge we see a landscape with 58   specifically Dutch features. Rembrandt has built up the little picture with great skill. In the foreground is the canal with the water at a high level and geese and a boat passing through the lock. Behind the lock the water flows at a lower level; its depth is plainly indicated by the two people in and near the boat. The two figures lead the eye and mind up to the bridge standing high above them, and finally to the highest level — the beam of the bridge. All in all a model of the Dutch landscape, which owes its character so completely to the separation of land and water areas achieved by its inhabitants.

The landscape drawings made in the years after Saskia's death until about 1655 testify to the fact that the town of Amsterdam and domesticity afforded no consolation to Rembrandt and no means of recovery through drawing and meditation. During the years of his married life with Saskia he had paid homage to the young mother and the children in hundreds of drawings and had amassed thoughts and observations; but no drawing is known of little Titus, who outlived his mother. His childhood may have been overshadowed by the conflict between the elderly maid Geertje Dircx and the young housekeeper Hendrickje Stoffels, and Rembrandt probably did not want to record his everyday troubles in the reflective diary, which is what his drawings were for him. Nor did he any longer seek to gather dramatic situations and to give them psychological meaning. Rather, he grasped at commonplace expressions of melancholy or stoic *Pl. 78* import. He made two rapid sketches of a gipsy or Moorish girl wearing a broad gaily coloured woven headshawl. With a most unlikely tool — perhaps a brush worn down to the holder — he had noted the bearing of the girl and the coloured pattern of the cloth, and then he had made the second sketch, transforming the headshawl into a kind of heavy coif concealing and protecting her from the world around.

In the wintry fields near Amsterdam he met the two shepherds who challenged him to *Pl. 122* meditation with the quill-pen by their composure and through the harmony of their physique and bearing.

He recorded on two sheets of paper, as he had done with the girl in the gay headshawl, a dead *Pl. 121* malefactor on the gallows with the instrument of her crime displayed beside her. His pupils too seem to have joined in this study, for one of their drawings, which exactly corresponds in subject matter to that of the master, has survived. The woman's corpse is wound round with spirals binding her to the gallows. Rembrandt has seen the contradiction between the puppetlike semblance of life in the position of the arm and the pendant body slumped on itself, and to reproduce the impression he has used the animating play of light with body shadows and lines and shadows cast by the horizontal beam.

Although it has been said that Rembrandt did not often make preparatory drawings for paintings or etchings, this does not imply that he was not concerned with painting problems while he was drawing. After all, Rembrandt depended for his livelihood primarily on commissions for portraits which he had to produce as paintings or etchings. In his forties he changed the character of his portraits. There was more space, the figure portrayed was smaller, and he 59 often introduced a stream of light flowing into the picture. This new form of portraiture was the result of experiments made and developed in drawings. The much scribbled over sheet

Pl. 117 of paper with the portrait of Secretary Lieven Coppenool is part of this experiment. Rembrandt had at first used framing lines to define the relation of the figure to the space. He made two etchings and a painting of van Coppenool, but there is no direct connection between them and the drawings.

Rembrandt introduced his new idea into a number of portraits, but his patrons seem rarely to have been pleased with this less representational form.

Pl. 123 In his country house, with its nearby trees, an Amsterdam gentleman sits on the edge of a bed by an open window relaxing unceremoniously after his day's work and life in the city. A sense of peace pervades the scene. In the drawing, the welcome shade in the room contrasts with the brilliant sunshine outside and completes the feeling of well-being.

Pl. 124 A study made in Rembrandt's studio seems to be constructed in a similar way. A woman, serving as model, is bathing the upper part of her bare body in sunlight during a pause in her work. For studio purposes the lower half of the high window is covered, a curtain serves further to regulate the light. The rays of the sun, so directed, fall on the woman's body with great intensity, almost dissolving the outlines of the figure and creating an aura of light, as though the onlooker's eyes were blinded by the brilliance of the sun-bathed skin.

Pls. 124 A 125 A In addition to the task of experimenting with the new form of relationship between the portrait and its setting, a new importance attaches to drawing from the nude in the studio. Nude models had always been necessary for the many pupils who had to learn how to portray the human body. Two exercises made by pupils give a glimpse into Rembrandt's studio in such a session. They show the master (then in his forties) correcting and advising, but not actually drawing the model. That accords with the fact that only a few drawings of nudes by Rembrandt before 1650 have come down to us, and what few there are have been made with a particular picture in view. However, it was not by chance that in the following year a number of completely naked women posed for him in the studio. In 1654 Rembrandt painted the Paris "Bathsheba," his most beautiful and most richly inspired homage to female beauty and in deference to the tragic conflicts to which she may be exposed. At this time, shortly before the end of his fiftieth year, the young Hendrickje Stoffels bore him a daughter, Cornelia, though they were not married. At this time his thoughts centred on the beauty of women as never before in his life.

Pl. 126 A splendid nude, drawn on parchment, vivid and yet soft in tone, shows a woman closely resembling the Paris "Bathsheba" in features and bearing. In contrast to the Bathsheba no

Pls. 125 & 128 thoughts are reflected in her face, which shows only the indifference of a good model. Now

Pls. 127 & 129 there alternate drawings of models in the studio which portray a precise pose and of others

Pl. 137 relaxed — resting or sleeping. Rembrandt at this period of his life has not in his creative work

overlooked the coquette who knows well how to display her physical attractions.

Certainly the models at this time would still be posed for his pupils, but he now no longer only corrected his pupils by pointing out faults, but worked with them, and added to the many acts of homage he paid to Eros in his fifties by lying in wait to capture the charm that the play of light on the rigid pose of the model now rounded out the contour, now dissolved the outline of the body.

Besides the numerous paintings for which Rembrandt in his fifties made sketches from life, are the drawings that represent Rembrandt as the head of his household. The only full-length *Pl. 131* self portrait shows him in the clothes he was accustomed to wear in the studio. In the critical look, the composed bearing and the obstinacy of the whole personality, one can imagine him at the approach and in the midst of the financial disaster and his awareness of his real worth as an outstanding painter, even though he has suffered disgrace in the eyes of the Amsterdam commercial world. Moreover, his work called for such deportment. Standing back from his easel, he compared his own bearing with that of the model seen in the mirror.

This critical examination shows how he could confront himself, far more than the detection of likeness, direction of lines, composition, and so forth. But if this same piercing glance in front of the easel, in front of the mirror, or in front of the model, was also his in everyday life, then the probing of these dark, lustreless eyes would have held at a distance all who were not embraced in his love.

Now at last the son Titus, already about fifteen years old, comes into the drawings. With the *Pl. 132* huge hat that the Dutch of that time seem only to have laid aside in church or before they went to bed, he has fallen into a light sleep in the studio. In unforgettable carefree strokes Rembrandt has sketched the boy. The fact that only a diagonal part – exactly half – of the sheet of paper has been used is almost as important as the lines.

On another occasion Titus is leaning, lost in thought, on the lower part of the housedoor, *Pl. 133* the upper part being open. In the play of light on the hard borderline between light and dark which Rembrandt had so often explored, flits again the feeling of security in the house and under the hat.

Titus worked with his father as a painter. The inventory of 1656 of Rembrandt's house and *Pl. 130* art possessions names three paintings by the then fifteen-year-old boy as the property of his father. Rembrandt drew his son while he was working in the studio – the face carefully with the brush, the moving hands with the broad reed-pen; then with a worn down brush or something similar he has rapidly, but with absolute sureness, washed in the outlines of the body, the stool and the drawing desk. It is just the differences in the tools used for drawing that give the impression that the boy is shuffling his feet, that his body is restless, yet the hands are under control and the mind is disciplined.

The portrait of Titus leaning on the housedoor (Pl. 133) has an antecedent in Rembrandt's *Pl. 134* work. In 1650/51 Rembrandt drew a girl in a similar position; a corresponding painting 61

(National Museum, Stockholm) bears the date 1651. Out of a dark depth, which here seems to indicate the hall of the house, Rembrandt the painter lets the light create shapes and colours. The malerisch (painterly) conception is found again in a line portrait of Hendrickje Stoffels a

Pl. 135 few years later. Thoughtfully Hendrickje leans against the door. Broad brushstrokes create a disturbing shadow around the young woman. In the drawing the darkness is less spatial, far more dynamic, like an oppressive conflict which the woman must clarify in thought and will.

Pls. 135 In this sharpening perception, in order to introduce a reflective-composed reality into a battle
136 between the powers of light and darkness, Rembrandt, in his sixtieth year, paid his final tribute to the beauty of women. With vigorous strokes of the vibrating shadows he made the woman's body appear to be a creation of light itself, dogmatically dull in some drawings, incomparably

Pl. 138 enchanting in others where he, as earlier in the drawing of Hendrickje (Pl. 135) activated the darkness and allows it to envelope the form like a husk so that the force of the light pierces

Pl. 138 through it all the more triumphantly.

Many of the drawings which Rembrandt made in his last creative period — in his fifties and sixties — show the interplay of thoughts which he expressed in his large paintings. The drawings are not exercises or variations, rather they date or emphasise an event. His drawings become ever more monosyllabic and reveal a specific idea in visual form. One can imagine him recording something hastily, often as it were in a kind of shorthand. One seems to detect such a "note" connected in thought with the story of Joseph and Potiphar's wife, of which Rembrandt made

Pl. 144 two large paintings in 1655 (Hermitage, Leningrad, and Museum Berlin Dahlem). The drawing shows an embarrassed but smiling youth with a hat in his hand, stepping back through a narrow

Pl. 142 open door where a woman stands in his way. Slandered by Potiphar's wife, Joseph was thrown into prison. There his fate was changed by his ability to interpret dreams. Rembrandt drew Joseph as a calm calculator, counting off on his fingers the explanation of the three things which his fellow-prisoners — the king's head baker and the king's head butler — had told them about their dreams. The figures are just sketched in; nothing further is said about their emotions of joy, surprise or horror. Rembrandt can now express "destiny" in drawing as no one before him had been able to do in the fine arts. There can be no doubt that the seated man is the head butler for whom Joseph has predicted freedom and good fortune, that the standing, bearded man must be the head baker, filled with the presentiment of death.

Pl. 143 The hasty, undisciplined drawing of Christ on the Mount of Olives with an attendant angel suggests that this was intended only as a preparatory sketch for a compositional picture. And indeed what has been thought out here has been introduced into the etching on the same theme

Pl. 141 which Rembrandt engraved c. 1657 (Bartsch 45). The sketch is in the shorthand style of Rembrandt's later years and has been rounded out into a composition based on the story of Judith, whom Holofernes takes to his bed. The artist has not followed the text of the Apocrypha closely

62 — this refers to hangings — and so has not made clear where the waking girl finds herself.

At this time, about 1655, Rembrandt's thoughts have turned again to an old problem, in a Pl. 150 large painting of Manoah's Offering. He has thought out afresh the possibility of hastily changing a seeming mortal into an angel or how a celestial being may suddenly reveal itself. Perhaps at this time he did not have in mind the departure of Tobias or the return of Manoah. The rich architectural surroundings with the domed building in the background and the bounding semicircle sketched in by Rembrandt would seem more suited to the announcement of the birth of John the Baptist to Zacharias as he performed his duties in the Temple. At all events this idea was changed by a pupil or by a copyist, who took the kneeling woman from another of Rembrandt's drawings of Manoah's Offering and placed her in the compositional picture.

To the Paris "Bathsheba" train of thought belongs clearly the framed picture of the scene Pl. 155 where the Prophet Nathan appeals to the conscience of King David. The prophet accuses the king of his sin in taking Bathsheba from her husband, Uriah, and of sending the husband to destruction. Ancient wisdom and human weakness seem to confront one another here. Rembrandt has fashioned the prophet on the lines of a bust of Homer which stood in his house together with similar busts of Socrates and Aristotle.

More and more there comes into Rembrandt's drawings, as also into the paintings, a sublimity of thought and feeling, achieved with the least possible expenditure of facial expression or gesture. So Rembrandt often shows the same emotional complex beloved by high baroque by quite contrary means.

The appearance of God to Abraham, drawn by Rembrandt in his fifties, shows the Lord God Pl. 159 attended by two floating figures, and over his head is a bird with outstretched wings. God appears to Abraham as a frail old man who must be led, but at the same time with a youthful countenance. The patriarch does not bow down to the vision, he seems moved neither by fear nor humility, but is completely overpowered and lies as though slain, his face hidden in his hands. Only by the position of the feet does Rembrandt make it clear that no dead man lies here. Rembrandt places God and his two attendants above and in front of entangled feathery strokes, so that the central figure stands out clear and calm, and, because of the economy of the lines, almost incorporeal. The bust in the dark niche must certainly have possessed some special significance, but it is difficult to recognise an association of thought here.

Rembrandt made the drawing of the Flight into Egypt in 1653, and it may have been influen- Pl. 149 ced by the fact that at the beginning of that year Christoffel Thije was pressing for payment of a debt of 8,500 guilders and threatening to recover the money by the sale of Rembrandt's house. From here the train of thought led to the parable of the Good Samaritan, which he had drawn Pl. 148 several times, but which he now grappled with anew. In this drawing the Samaritan unemotionally but gently tends the wounded man. Rembrandt has introduced a new thought — the ennobling of custom by good example: the practical street lad who has interrupted his errand to calm down the mule by holding it, and in so doing has developed a sense of responsibility. 63

Rembrandt has also depicted an inner change in the innkeepers since he made the earlier drawing of them. They have gained something in feeling, but are sharply contrasted with the Samaritan. The man is emotional; the wife reflective. He stands at the door, senile, obviously upset, without a thought of being helpful. The old woman thinks in advance what a burden the wounded man would be in the house, and she would like to shut the door, which she holds with her hand, in the face of the unfortunate stranger.

Pl. 151 The story of Daniel in the lion's den belongs, like the parable of the Good Samaritan, belongs to subjects which Rembrandt used pictorially as lessons for humanity. When he wanted just to make a drawing based on such a theme, but not to use it for an etching or painting that everybody might see, then he felt free to introduce his Amsterdam neighbours into his thoughts and work. Daniel was condemned to the gruesome death laid down in the letter of the law that his enemies had cunningly evoked from King Darius. The final lesson that Rembrandt had to teach was that lions are more humane than people. Unfortunately the splendid picture is ruined by the fawning lion in the middle, where in the course of time a "worthless" piece of drawing has forced its way through the masking white (body colour) which Rembrandt had painted *Pls. 152 153* over it. The powerful drawings of lions that Rembrandt had made from living animals at every opportunity which presented itself, have been used successfully in this picture. Rembrandt's four lions here are the embodiment of affection, indifference, mistrust and anger.

Though in considering Rembrandt's drawings it has often been said that he transferred biblical stories into the everyday light of contemporary Holland and brought the foundations of Christian humanism before the eyes in apparently everyday happenings, then one should also consider a different relationship between the artist and his environment in his maturity. It so happened that Rembrandt now often saw the commonplace happenings around him in a biblical light, that is in the opposite way in which they had been seen in the early part of the sixteenth century and had been portrayed in netherlandish art. Thus he saw how two men were trying to retrieve some object that had fallen into the water from the bank of a canal. Then he called to mind the miraculous deed of the prophet Elisha, when he made the iron swim so that *Pl. 88* it should not be lost. He had earlier depicted a "miracle" of the prophet Elijah, now he dressed the old Dutchmen in biblical garments, gave one of them homerish-prophetish features and left the "miracle" scarcely recognisable: everyday happenings in a biblical light, as earlier biblical episodes in everyday life. Often now Rembrandt's drawings are so calm and matter-of-fact that *Pl. 160* it is difficult to follow his thoughts. The lying-in room built up in cubes seems to relate to the birth of John the Baptist. The priests on the right have come to name the child, and the father who had been struck dumb writes down the name John and immediately regains his power of speech.

Pl. 161 Entirely different is the clear and powerfully constructed drawing of a scene in an inn where 64 a woman is placing food before a knight and his two companions. Here Rembrandt has introduced a biblical connotation. The reflective young soldier has become King Saul, who has summoned the witch of Endor to raise up the spirit of Samuel from the dead, and now he learns that he will be overthrown and his people conquered.

Gloomily he sits by the fire, while the woman (who does not look at all like a witch) serves a quickly prepared meal. Note how Rembrandt has built up the cubes of table, stools and people with straight, deep brush strokes, and has filled in the shadows with an almost dry brush.

On the other hand, in the drawing of a boat, Rembrandt has certainly not seen Jesus in a *Pl. 162* storm on the lake of Galilee. With falling square sail and through surging waves, a boat runs into the wind. This is no storm; the boat and the people are in no danger; another boat sails near it. This is one of the very few drawings that Rembrandt made of fishermen and sailors. *Pl. 163* It is in the same category as the angler on the dyke and the two shepherds. *Pl. 122*

It is hard to follow Rembrandt's thoughts in the drawing of the return of the Prodigal Son *Pl. 164* which he made in his later years. As it appears today, Rembrandt finished it and enclosed it with framing lines. The impressive architecture with the gate and the draw-bridge show the magnificence of the father's house, to which the son returns ill and ragged. Rembrandt first drew the son alone, as he collapses on the threshold of the house. A woman in the doorway recognises the young master with horror. Only later did Rembrandt add the father, placing him on the step and near the seat by the housedoor which he had already sketched. With the silhouette of the devoted, forgiving old man, with the grasp of the son as though he were dronwing, he brings to the pitiable scene the ethical content of his late work, which speaks of pity, humanity and tolerance. Rembrandt painted the same subject – the Return of the Prodigal Son – as his last work, in the year of his death (Hermitage, Leningrad).

It has already been said that Rembrandt signed only a few of his drawings with his name. They were not intended for sale, and seem rarely to have been given as presents. Many people, however, kept of albums to which they asked friends and acquaintances to contribute; particularly travellers, students and scholars naturally it was to a great extent the name of the contributor that mattered, and when one was a Rembrandt it was particularly sought after. In 1634 Rembrandt drew a small study of a head in an album kept by the traveller Burchard Grossman, Junior, of Weimar. In 1661 he honoured Jacob Heyblock, a minister of the Dutch church in Amsterdam with a small drawing. For this album he chose a well-known subject which he had painted earlier, almost at the beginning of his independent career: the presentation of the child Jesus in the Temple and Simeon's recognition (Kunsthalle, Hamburg, c. 1628). Simeon had received a divine promise that he should not die before he had seen the Messiah, and here he is portrayed at the moment of revelation and is communicating the spiritual signi-ficance to Mary and Joseph. Deep shadow seems to be dispersed by the light that rests on *Pl 174* Simeon's hands. Mary, on the left, with the halo of motherhood over her head, plainly believes. Joseph, at her side, appears overshadowed and seems to be profoundly astonished. Indescribable, 65 however, is the appearance of Simeon who realises that the revelation of the Messiah means for him imminent death.

Here Rembrandt drew with the highest spiritual force the death mask of one cut off from life in a moment of ecstacy. Nowhere else has a mystical experience been so profoundly interpreted visually as this recognition of the Saviour by Simeon which brought with it his long-desired death. For Rembrandt these lines on a small piece of paper, about a hundred square centimetres in size, are the last word. Not that he never drew again, but he never again attained such perfection with such slender means: three human faces, pen, brush and a little coloured fluid.

It is particularly difficult to follow Rembrandt's thought associations in individual studies and ideas for composition during the last creative years of his life. The episodes in his late drawings are no longer dialectic, with conversation, expressions that convey the sense of the words and emphasis on the main theme underlined by the indifference of subsidiary figures; now each single figure is of direct importance to the main theme, but each in a different way. The late style of Rembrandt's drawing and the thoughts that lead to it have already been analysed in the "Good Samaritan" (Pl. 148).

Pl. 167 The drawing of two men, the one sad, worn-out and old — a Peter type with drawn sword — supported and being led away, conveys a direct, understandable message. But it is difficult to decide whether Rembrandt has seen an everyday episode in a biblical light and perhaps connected it in his mind with Peter's third denial to the servant of the High Priest.

Pl. 166 At the beginning of his sixtieth year Rembrandt had jotted down in the apparently rough and ready manner of his late style of drawing two pairs of figures. In one sketch a stumbling old man is guided by a youth. In the other sketch to the right the youth has subsequently been blotted out and made useless by masking; it did not convey Rembrandt's idea that both figures should appear to be walking unsteadily. In this case it can be said with certainty what thoughts were connected with the drawings. In the Tobias story, which Rembrandt returned to again and again, each time with a new point of view, it was said that the old, blind Tobias wanted to hurry to greet his returning son, but stumbled and called a servant to his help. A comparison of the variations in the two drawings of the old man makes one realise the sharpness with which Rembrandt could now define mental and spiritual processes. His artistic achievements could no longer be expressed more vividly in words.

This late style has an exquisite certainty; yet there is a seeming indifference in non-essential details. In the large picture, framed in line by Rembrandt himself, of Peter raising Tabitha from the dead, the head of the apostle remains unforgettable but also incomprehensible in so far as the earnest appearance and the powerful look of the Peter-type seem contrived.

Pl. 168 In fact the carelessly drawn bed canopy and the comic baroque figure that supports it, leads one to think of play-acting.

The loose lines, made with a clumsy, very dry tool, is typical of his late draughtsmanship. Great clarity in the building up of the scene often accompanied by barely suggested details is *Pl. 165* also characteristic of it. Nevertheless, the late composition of the owner of the vineyard and his labourers is no less profound than the earlier ones (Pls. 92/93). With complete directness, in contrast to baroque, Rembrandt proclaims essential truths of humanity, of care for the needy, and of the weakness, doubt and selfishness of men.

The last official commissions came to Rembrandt in the years around 1660. The director of the Amsterdam Cloth-makers Guild ordered a group portrait of their Syndics, the officials responsible for examining the quality of the Guild members' products. Rembrandt was by no means forgotten, even though since about 1643 Bartholomäus van der Helst had become the painter of group portraits to whom the rich, proud and class-conscious merchants of Amsterdam turned. Possibly the craft guilds were more conservative than the volunteer defence corps and so Rembrandt seemed more suitable to them. This is not the place to evaluate the painting of the Syndics ("Staalmeisters"). (Reichsmuseum, Amsterdam.)

In a drawing connected with this theme Rembrandt had "tried out" the main group. The *Pl. 169* excellent idea of painting the Syndics in conversation with a viewer of the picture had not yet occurred to Rembrandt when he was making the drawing; here the Syndics are still in conference, and they have not been raised to the higher level opposite the onlooker. Although the drawing is quite clearly only a preliminary to the complete composition, the likeness to the painting is evident.

The second important commission – the historical picture for the Amsterdam City Hall, and *Pl. 172* the tragic loss to mankind of this monumental work of western art – has already been referred to in Rembrandt's life. The preparatory draft for the 30 square metre picture shows the care taken by Rembrandt over the smallest details. The important role which he conceded to the architecture in his composition shows the great consideration with which he approached this vast project. The arched hall in which the conspiracy of Julius Civilis was planned is unmistakably and wilfully like the entrance to the reception room in the City Hall. So what took place in a different world now seems to be related to the actual surroundings, but the idea behind it and the means by which the episode was recorded were clearly an intellectual and artistic achievement quite above the onlookers' comprehension.

The great heights which Rembrandt had reached with this magnificent picture for the town *Pl. 170* hall can be seen in other drawings of the late period. "Noah's Ark" was not a picture that would have been suitable for the rooms in the City Hall in the vicinity of the "Conspiracy" both because of its subject matter and the way in which it was painted. Rembrandt drew the arches as though they were a vaulted deck construction of a ship lying alongside the quay. A wide timber "bridge" leads up to the ship, and Noah's sons with their wives and children are going aboard just like ship's passengers in Rembrandt's own day, while the curious onlookers stand by 67 gossiping. All that has been set down with a quite clumsy implement yet with the greatest precision; the bent knee and the hesitating step of the man with the load on his shoulder, the heaviness of the woman holding a bundle in both arms, the old woman who has nothing to carry, but instead is looking after the child. Over all is the most beautiful spatial clarity. The way leads over the bridge to the wide open landing gate and into the sucking darkness of the entrance to the protective house structure.

It was a fitting tribute to the magnificence of Rembrandt's late work that he apparently received a commission to paint a lifesize equestrian picture befitting the growing aristocratic tendency of Amsterdam society. The subject itself was not new to him. In 1655 he had painted on a small scale the Polish rider, and about four years later the lifesize monumental portrait of the Amsterdam merchant, Frederick Richel, on horseback (National Gallery, London). This time it was to be a lady on horseback setting out on a hawking expedition, again lifesize. Hawking was a new theme in Dutch painting and, we may assume, at that time a new pastime for Dutch society. This kind of hunting is avowedly an artistocratic pursuit, more a gruesome sport than true hunting, since no useful booty is obtained. Its fascination is really in watching the battle between the trained falcon and the wild bird. Although no exact research seems to have been made into the hunt in Holland in the seventeenth century, one can perhaps detect in the adoption of this sport of princes and noblemen a symptom of foreign influence and the spreading of feudal tendencies. Rich burghers clamoured after titles of nobility and country seats; in the City Hall, however, they wanted Manius Curius Dentatus portrayed at his plain meal of turnips, refusing the costly gift of the Samnites. As far as Rembrandt is concerned, the feudal attribute of the falcon emerged for the first time in 1643 in a commissioned picture (Duke of Westminster, London). Whether "The Falconer" which he painted in 1661 (Museum Göteburg) was commissioned or not remains an open question. Perhaps Rembrandt has here seized on a fashionable theme to show what, with thought, he could make of it.

Pl. 173 Related to "The Falconer" of 1661 is the drawing of the setting out for the hunt. The figure is riding astride the horse, but the features, the fact that the horse is led on a rein by a boy and the gentle movements of the animal suggest that the rider could be a woman. The picture is relatively simple in composition, but only the last phase of the drawing should be considered – the stable boy with the horse in profile on the right does not belong to it. With only a few changes in the figures the picture could just as well be of the Holy Family on the flight to Egypt. The commission, the source of which is unknown, stipulates a painting at least three metres high. Yet scarcely anything was said about the aristocratic, fashionable falconry. Lady, hawk, mount and servant – as a result of Rembrandt's study of street group composition – are patently dependent on one another, while their individuality is made apparent in details like the carriage of the head. These are the thoughts that motivated Rembrandt as he made and altered

68 his preparatory drawings.

Finally, Diana and Acteon, one of the last of the surviving drawings by Rembrandt: this belongs to the fashionable baroque which Rembrandt subdued to his will. In the Renaissance Diana and her bathing nymphs provided the desired pretext for studying and painting the female nude. To the courtly baroque the scene from Ovid's "Metamorphoses" appealed because of its sensuality. Surprised chastity, typified by the goddess Diana and her nymphs, must be made clear in enchanting and diverse bodily movements. Roughly thirty years earlier Rembrandt had treated the same subject in an audacious painting (in private possession Rhede/Westphalia) as a parody on gods and mortals. Now he was incited by an Italian engraving in the baroque style, but saw his task in complete opposition to it. He decided, through his intellect, to etherial- Pl. 17. ise the piquante, fashionable theme. He eschewded outward signs of shame and fear on the part of Diana and her female following. In free, relaxed manner the women follow the progressive stages in the bewitchment of the hunter Acteon whom Diana has changed into a stag. From the man Acteon they had turned away; but now that he has lost his human form they approach him with curiosity. The same thing happens with the huntsman's hounds. So far he had been their master; now they note how the man they had feared and obeyed is changing into a prey for them. Still in conflict with their instincts, Rembrandt lets them turn insidiously against the Acteon stag. In this way Rembrandt ignores the erotic excitement of the story, but follows another train of thought — the tragic meeting of the harmless mortal with the goddess who, with a smile, with a glance over her shoulder, condemns the hunter to a gruesome death, to be torn in pieces by his hounds. Emphatically, Rembrandt has separated the fields of the gods from those of the mortals by giant trees. Only spiritual powers can span the boundaries. Though the drawing is perhaps the last one to survive, it would be wrong to suppose that it marks the end of Rembrandt's mental probing and composition, and to look upon him as a resigned fatalist. However much self-revelation may lie in his drawings, the works of his maturity still proclaim what a hundred years later was known as "education for humanity." In his drawing of the lady setting out on a hawking expedition he ignored the horse- and hunt-allure, and in Acteon he brought to the fore the warning of Goethe's Iphigenie: "The gods fear the human race."

Having tried to evaluate Rembrandt's drawings during some forty years of creative work in line and contemplation, there remains the question of their deeper meaning. The drawings, like Leonardo's research and discovery, had no message for his contemporaries because they were inaccessible to the general public. Only indirectly through the paintings and etchings, in which the results of the preliminary drawing and thought were partially apparent, could his message reach a wider circle of people in his own day. How his views were received and how far they were understood, cannot be discussed here in detail.

It has often been said that Rembrandt's work as artist and thinker succeeded in that he strove above all else to understand his fellow creatures (their nature, character, state, disposition, conduct, demeanour, bearing, manners, affairs, organisation and so forth. It is not by chance that we recognise in accounts of his life the family feeling, understanding, and unselfish love, and the consideration that members of the little Rembrandt family showed to one another. Rembrandt lived with his own according to his perception. If we seek this perception in his drawings, then we find them in youth first in the study of changing emotions. In contrast to his artist predecessors, Rembrandt did not begin with types of people. He sought to show how joy, sadness, pain, anger express themselves differently in every sort of man. It does not happen, as in sixteenth-century art, that an angry man belongs to one particular type, but the effect of anger expresses itself in different ways in every type. Rembrandt complicated his self-imposed task by introducing the significance of outward symbols such as hats, caps, turbans or headscarves to support his contention. If this appears to be at first a youthful lack of independence, a by-product of baroque art-teaching, it is possible on closer inspection to detect the kernel of wisdom that took root in Rembrandt's understanding of men. Rembrandt included headdress in the visual expression of feelings, because it played an important role in class consciousness and self-esteem. The distinctions which he introduced into his drawn and painted self-portraits were that a man in a high hat comported himself differently from one wearing a turban or flat cap, that the same emotion was expressed differently in the cap-wearer than by a man in a baretta.

To such observation of individuals he soon added the group, which he built up from speaker and listener. There was always just one storyteller or messenger of good or bad news. The group was placed over against him to permit a differentiation in the reactions of the hearers. From 1629 until 1633 the witnesses of the raising of Lazarus (Etching, Bartsch 73) or the Descent from the Cross (Etching, Bartsch 81) reacted in very much the same way. Rembrandt discovered (as shown in his drawings) in the following period from about 1635 to 1642 how differently he must draw or paint to represent human feelings more accurately. At that time the uninhibited world of the child and mother opened out to him. That led him to mistrust the outward signs of adult emotions. He saw how much of such outward emotion was pose, exhibitionism and "theatre"; he recognised too that so far his own visual interpretations of feelings were false. At the same time in order to arrive at a true understanding of the pose, he went, for schooling, to showgrounds, theatrical productions and to the markets where salesmen "pushed" their wares. While he made a study of theatricality he detected the falsity in the outward expression of ordinary people; he tried to avoid the false and to replace it by authentic expressions. Through such studies he ripened during the years between 1640 and 1650 into the sage and the teacher of mankind. What he worked out through meditation in drawing and expressed in paintings and etchings, was the knowledge that the man of his time was no longer "the evil one," "the true man," "the betrayer," "the believer," but that the potentialities for each could be present in everyone. In this way Rembrandt achieved the profound means of expression which in our review of the later drawings we have sought to describe, when the doubting, the hesitant, acted under compulsion against commonsense, and because of their mixed emotions conflicts ensued between "must" and "will." Here astonishment was mingled with fear, obedience had a savour of revolt, hate was mingled with love, pity with self-seeking, or belief with doubt.

So Rembrandt recognised and made recognisable in his drawings the men of the new age, the informed and therefore doubting. This was certainly much too soon for his contemporaries to appreciate and much more easily understood by generations hundreds of years after his death, conditioned by the advancement of humanity, and the education of the masses. Rembrandt had not become old-fashioned in his forties, as had sometimes been said, on the contrary, he was far advance of his time.

The teaching of Calvanism, paramount in Holland took as the basis for conduct the religious laws of the Old Testament, and through its teaching of predestination of human fate by divine, implacable will, sought to excuse every deed as preordained. Rembrandt's knowledge of human nature, as documented in his drawings and some paintings, in no way corresponded with this view. Where laws from an earlier stage of mankind's development laid down in the Old Testament still had validity, where the deed was already pre-judged, there was no room for indecision, for doubt, or for indulgence as Rembrandt revealed them. Drunken and brawling peasants behaved according to their destiny; the arrogant company of Captain Bicker was just as correctly painted by Bartholomäus van der Helst (1643, Reichsmuseum, Amsterdam) as the richly dressed Director of the Armshouse by Ferdinand Bol (1657, Reichsmuseum, Amsterdam) in front of the coffer. Rembrandt's Syndics were not in step with their time because they were listening to opinions from outside. It was not fitting that a king possessed of evil spirits, yet sent by God, should be moved by a simple shepherd lad playing upon a harp. (Rembrandt, David plays before Saul, c. 1665, Mauritshuis, The Hague.) Poor people recognised and approved the dignity and superiority of the directors of armshouses, so that scenes showing the emotion of the father on the return of his lost, dissipated son (Rembrandt, 1668/69, Hermitage, Leningrad) were not understood.

First the philosophers, foremost among them Descartes, proclaimed doubt to be the starting point in the search for truth and human reason to be the foundation of knowledge. When their teaching took root among the rising middle classes in the eighteenth century and grew to be their mental armour in the "Storm and Stress," men arrived at the position that Rembrandt had attained a hundred years earlier. Humanity, brotherhood, understanding and forgiveness, respect for the individuality of other people, questing instead of belief, that was what Rembrandt had at last thought out in his drawings and sought in his works of art to pass on to the minds and hearts of his contemporaries and posterity.

"For all artists: give nourishment to a still undefined curiosity, respond to an as yet unformulated desire, so that one who is still a child today will be astonished tomorrow to find me on his path." **71**

Abbreviations:

Ben.: Otto Benesch, The Drawings of Rembrandt, volume
I-VI. London, no date (1954-1957).

Val.: Wilhelm Valentiner, Rembrandt, The Master's Drawings,
volume I Stuttgart, no date (1925),
volume II Stuttgart, no date (1933),
volume III not published.

HdG.: C. Hofstede de Groot, Rembrandt's Hand Drawings,
Haarlem 1906.

HB.: E. Haverjamp-Begemann, review by Benesch, The
Drawings by Rembrandt in "Art Chronicle" XIV 1961
page 10 and the following pages,
page 50 f.p., page 85 f.p.

A

Leonardo da Vinci, Study of horses, lions and men. Pen and Ink. Windsor, Royal Library.

B

Albrecht Dürer, Study for a St.Christopher presentation. Pen 228/407. Berlin, Kupferstichkabinett.

C, D, E

Rembrandt, Three studies of the work on "Ecce Homo". Compare to plates 43/44.

1

Self portrait, bust. About 1627/28. Pen, Bistre, Brush and Indian Ink. 127×95 mm. London, British Museum.
Ben. Vol. I. No. 53. Figure 60. (1627/28). Val. 657. (Ca. 1629). HdG. 895. (Ca. 1629).

2

Old man with book. Seated profile to the right, full length. Red and black chalk, heightened with white on reddish paper on the right 8 mm strip has been added to the paper. 295×210 mm. Berlin, Kupferstichkabinett.
Study for the painting of 1628. Two philosophers disputing. Melbourne, National Gallery of Victoria.
Ben. Vol. I. No. 7. Figure 10. (1628). HdG. 112. (Ca. 1630/31). Rotterdam Catalogue 1956 No. 7.

3

Study of an archer. About 1627. Red chalk heightened with white on partially reddish toned paper. The back of the archer and the quiver have been heightened with a brush. Inscribed by a later hand; Van Segen (Referring to Ludwig von Siegen). 306×162 mm. Dresden, Kupferstichkabinett.
Ben Vol. I. No. 3. Figure 1. (Ca. 1627). Val. 795 A. (Ca. 1629).

4

Old man with his arms extended. About 1629. Black chalk. 256×193 mm. Dresden, Kupferstichkabinett.
Study in reverse for the figure of St. Peter in the etching St. Peter and St. John healing the paralysed at the Gate of the Temple. Bartsch 95.
Ben. I. No. 12. Figure 13. (Ca. 1629). Val. 530. (Ca. 1629). HdG. 233. (Ca. 1630).

5

Polish officer – Full length. About 1630/31. Red Chalk. 255×185 mm. Leningrad, Hermitage (Inv. 14946).
Ben. I. No. 45. Figure 49. (Ca. 1630/31).

6

Bearded old man in high cap. Looking out of a door hatch, and resting both hands on it. About 1633. Quill and reed pen, brush, washes, bistre, corrected with white. 174×105 mm. Dresden, Kupferstichkabinett.
Ben. Vol. II. No. 216. Figure 235. (Ca. 1633). HdG. 238. (Ca. 1635).

7

Study of a woman asleep. Seated in profile to right, her left foot on a stove. About 1632/33. Black chalk. Upper right portion repaired (93 × 110 mm). 250 × 220 mm. Dresden, Kupferstichkabinett.

The drawing is not a figure study, but a space composition. It has since been reduced to a figure alone because of the damage to the edges.

Ben. Vol. II. No. 196. Figure 212. (Ca. 1632/33). HdG. (Ca. 1628/30).

8

Study for a St. Jerome Repentant. About 1623/33. Pen and Bistre. 150 × 114 mm. Wroclaw, Ossolineum.

Ben. Vol. I. No. 67. Figure 68. (Ca. 1632/33).

9

Old man and young woman walking. About 1632/33. Pen and Bistre. 149 × 98 mm. Dresden, Kupferstich-kabinett.

Ben. Vol. II. No. 202. Figure 216. (Ca. 1632/33). HdG. 272. (Ca. 1629). HB. p. 20.

10

Group of four orientals standing. With differing head dress. About 1632/33. Pen and Bistre wash 144 × 123 mm. Budapest, Museum of Fine Arts.

Ben. Vol. II. No. 210. Figure 229. HdG. 1384.

11

The circumcision of Jesus. About 1632/33. Pen and Bistre; with number '4' the upper corners rounded. 205 × 223 mm. The drawing gives the impression of being a copy, however, it is the wash that weakens the tones. England, in private Collection.

Ben. Vol. I. No. 72. Figure 78. Val. 306. (Ca. 1633). HdG. 211.

12

The departure of the prodigal son. About 1632/33. Pen and Bistre, wash. The upper corners rounded. 192 × 275 mm. In the doorway is a grey-brown watery brush wash, which has partially dissolved the pen strokes. The blurred form to the left of the horse's head is by another hand. Dresden, Kupferstichkabinett.

Ben. Vol. I. No. 81. Figure 85. (1632/33). Val. 383. (Ca. 1634). HdG. 217.

13

Tric-trac players. Two Lovers, and a man smoking a pipe behind them. About 1635. Pen and Bistre on paper, joined together in three vertical portions. 176 × 163 mm. Venice, Accademia.

Ben. Vol. II. No. 398. Figure 454. (Ca. 1635). Val. 772. (Ca. 1634). HdG. 1156. Rotterdam Catalogue No. 25 (1632/35).

14

Lot and the men of Sodom. Pen and Bistre with lighter brown overworkings. The overworkings consist of the formless hand on the head of the middle figure, and the strokes on his left shoulder and breast, the confused down strokes on the breast of the left hand figure, the cross strokes descending from the right sleeve to the ground, which give the figure depth and shadow. We cannot decide whether or not the overworking can be attributed to Rembrandt himself. This drawing, first published in 1956, was apparently in the same possession as Ben. 279, 313, 402, 442. We tell from the history of Lot, and see in the drawings, how Lot on the threshold of his house, defends his guests against the demands of the Sodomites, damned for their habits. Gen. 19, 4–8. The clothing of the people is indicative of their iniquity. Franz Menton also, in his engraving of the history of Lot and the Sodomites (Ca. 1610–15), vigorously differentiated between Lot and the people of Sodom.

(Hollstein: Dutch Etchings. Plate XIV. p. 8). We do not incline to the opinion that Lot is inviting in the two Angels (1. Gen. 19, 2–3) since Rembrandt's Angels are always depicted with wings, and in any case the expression and the gesticulations of the old man could in no way be interpreted as an invitation. (W. Sumowski in the Scientific Journal of the Humboldt-University, Berlin, VI. 1956/7, p. 257). 205×161 mm. Leipzig, Museum.

Not in Ben. Val. or HdG.

15

Manius Curius Dentatus refuses the gifts of the Samnites. About 1633/34. Pen and Bistre, wash. 145×185 mm. Plut. Cata 2. 2. Cicero, Cato 55. Valerius Maximus IV. 3. 5. An engraving (in reverse) inscribed 'Cabinet de Mr. Uilebroek' by B. Picart. Impostures Innocentes, Amsterdam 1734. I. (I. J. de Claussin, Supplement 1828. p. 157 No. 61). A copy in the Rijksprentenkabinet, Amsterdam. Valentiner 583. Collection: Leningrad, Academy of Fine Arts 1832–1932. According to Falck, who considers this drawing a copy, the outlines are traced for transfer. A drawing of the same subject is in the Albertina, listed there as by G. van der Eeckhout. H. Schneider has recognized it as the preparatory drawing by F. Bol for his painting in the City Hall of Amsterdam. In the Albertina drawing the compositional setting of the three figures of the present drawing was used, but thoroughly transformed into the style of the pupil, (Hans Schneider, "F. Bol als Monumentalmaler im Amsterdamner Stadthaus", Jahrb. d. Preuss. Kunstslgen 47. (1926) p. 77. Fig. 7). The high quality of the drawing excludes the possibility of its being a copy. Its style points to the studies of Orientals done about 1633, particularly to Ben. No. 85. Warsaw, University Library. Count S. Potocki Collection. (T. 1155. No. 8).

Ben. Vol. I. No. 86. Figure 94. (1633/34).

16

Lot and his daughters after the destruction of Sodom. About 1636. Pen and Bistre. 152×191 mm. A painting according to Hofstede de Groot by an unknown pupil (perhaps Jacob Backer) who made use of the present drawing, is in the Rath collection, Budapest (as Christoffel Paudiss). Bredius Feest-Bundel. Pl. No. 27. The seduction of Lot by his daughters (1. Gen 19, 31–35) was a popular theme in the 16th and 17th centuries, and was very often painted. Rembrandt's drawing bears a close relation to No. 14. Weimar, Goethe Nationalmuseum. Collection: Goethe (L. 1087 cut off).

Ben. Vol. I. No. 128. Figure 141. (Ca. 1636). Val. 45. (Ca. 1635). HdG. 528. (Ca. 1635).

17

Study for a blinding of Samson. About 1635. Pen and Bistre. 147×202 mm. Valentiner connects this drawing with the painting of 1636. The Blinding of Samson. Frankfurt-on-Main (HdG. 33, Bredius 501). A drawing connected with the Samson subject and clearly showing the style of 1636 is already known; the sketch in Dijon. It differs in style somewhat from the present drawings, which correspond more closely to the works of 1635. Also the figures approaching the entangled group with quick feline movements seem not to be those of bulky warriors clad in steel as we see them in the painting of 1636. It is suggested, therefore, that the painting might be connected with the group of Callisto struggling with her companions in the painting of 1635. Diana bathing dG. 200. Mark. Dresden, Kupferstichkabinett.

Ben. Vol. I. No. 93. Figure 103. (Ca. 1935). HdG. 263. Val. 807.

18

Group of musicians listening to flute player. 135×154 mm. Pen and wash. Donnington-Priory, Newbury, Berkshire, Captain G. M. Garthorne Hardy.

Ben. Vol. II. No. 399. Figure 452. (Ca. 1635). HdG. 983. (Ca. 1635). Val. 769. (Ca. 1630). Rotterdam Catalogue 1956, No. 24. (1632/35).

19

Cottage with landing place, and a row of trees by a canal. About 1636. Pen and Wash. 213×190 mm. Weimar, Goethe Nationalmuseum.

Ben. Vol. II. No. 470. Figure 530. HdG. 535.

20

A dromedary, and two Orientals standing behind it. About 1633. Pen and Bistre. Some white body colour. 194×289 mm. Inscribed with signature and date by another hand: Drommedaris Rembrandt fecit 1633 Amsterdam. Bremen, Art Gallery (Missing since 1945).

Ben. Vol. II. No. 453. Figure 511. HB. p. 27.

21

Watch-dog sleeping in his kennel. About 1633. Pen and gallnut ink. Wash. 130×153 mm. Boston USA, Museum of Fine Arts.

Ben. Vol. II. No. 455. Figure 510.

22

Farm-house in sunlight. About 1636. Pen and Wash. Inscribed by a later hand. Rembrandt. 165×223 mm. (Etched by Joseph Schmidt.) Budapest, Museum of Fine Arts.

Ben. Vol. II. No. 463. Figure 523. HdG. 1393. Rotterdam Catalogue. No. 96a. (1635/39).

23

Court-yard of the same farm-house. Drawn some hours later. About 1636. Pen and Bistre, wash. 164×226 mm. A comparison of the shadow line of the corner of the house and the projecting roof gives an indication of the short time lapse between the two drawings. Budapest, Museum of Fine Arts.

Ben. Vol. II. No. 464. Figure 524. HdG. 1394. Rotterdam Catalogue No. 96b. (1635/39).

24

Self portrait. Half length. A Palette is hanging on the wall. About 1634. Pen and Bistre, wash, covered with white. The drawing has been overworked with great care by brush and the hard outlines have been toned down. Accentuations have been brought about, for example, the eyes, by leaving the original colour. Hofstede de Groot, followed by Valentiner, dated this drawing about 1645, much too late. Lilienfeld on the other hand by drawing comparisons with Self-Portraits of the late 1620's arrived at too early a date, Rosenberg came to a more correct result about 1635. 123×137 mm. Berlin, Kupferstichkabinett.

Ben. Vol. II. No. 432. Figure 488. Val. 663. HdG. 98.

25

Saskia sitting up in bed. About 1634. Pen and brush in bistre. The right cheek has been washed and heightened with a weak white. The dark left hand cheek contours are heightened in white. This white has, however, suffered severe oxidation. 150×138 mm. Dresden, Kupferstichkabinett.

Ben. Vol. II. No. 255. Figure 276. Val. 687. (Ca. 1636). HdG. 255. (Ca. 1635).

26

Two studies of Saskia asleep in bed, with her head on a pillow. About 1635. Pen and brush in bistre. Inscribed: Rymsdyk's Museum. 130×171 mm. New York, Pierpont Morgan Library.

Ben. Vol. II. No. 289. Figure 319. Val. 690. Rotterdam Catalogue 1956. No. 51. (1635/41).

27

Seated young woman with a baby, and an old woman looking at it. About 1636. Pen and bistre, cut off at the upper margin where the fragment of a sketch is visible. The great graphic artists before Rembrandt, such as Leonardo da Vinci and Dürer had no children. Leonordo da Vinci, in fact, had no family, nor do we hear of Dürer's wife Agnes having any children. In such a scene as this all artists of the 16th century had to fight against the "Anna Selbdritt' pattern. Rembrandt was one of the first artists, dating from his marriage, who portrayed his "Mother and Child" as anywhere near woman. 130×110 mm. Dresden, Kupferstichkabinett.

76   Ben. Vol. II. No. 304. Figure 343. HdG. 264. (No date.)

28

Nurse and child. About 1635. Red Chalk. 177×128 mm. Wroclaw, Ossolineum.
Ben. Vol. II. No. 278. Figure 305. HB. p. 24.

29

Woman carrying a child downstairs. Into the open air. About 1636. Pen and bistre, wash. 185×133 mm.
New York, Pierpont Morgan Library.
According to Benesch and others the drawing is of "Saskia carrying Rumbartus downstairs." However, this supposition cannot be defended. The child was baptised on the 15th December 1635, but the drawing was executed after the burial of a child of Rembrandt's, the date of which has been established as taking place on the 15th of February 1636. (Compare with Otto Benesch, "Rembrandt as a Draughtsman," London 1960. Cat. No. 21 p. 147.)
Ben. Vol., II. No. 313. Figure 347. Val. 675.

30

Studies of beggars and of an old woman with a crying child. About 1633/34. Pen and bistre, wash, some white body colour. 218×186 mm. Berlin, Kupferstichkabinett.
Ben. Vol. II. No. 218. Figure 240. HdG. 157. (Ca. 1635). Rotterdam Catalogue 1956. No. 44. (1635/37).

31

The widower. A man feeding a little child, the bust of the child sketched again twice. About 1636/37. Pen and bistre, wash. 173×142 mm. Copenhagen, Kobberstik Samling.
Ben. Vol. II. No. 345. Figure 401. HdG. 1013. (1643/45). HB. p. 26.

32

The naughty boy. About 1635. Pen and bistre, wash, white body colour, some black chalk in the old woman; light flesh colour; the left foot of the child retouched with a finger; inscribed by a later hand: Rembrandt. 206×143 mm. Berlin, Kupferstichkabinett.
Ben. Vol. II. No. 401. Figure 459. HdG. 140. (Ca. 1635). Val. 781. (Ca. 1636). HB. p. 27.

33

The rape of Ganymede. Two figures below, one of them aiming with a cross bow at the Eagle. 1635. Pen and bistre, wash. The corrections to the child's buttocks and to the triangular form of the left arm have been toned down with white body colour. The light watery wash has in parts dissolved the strokes of the eagle's wings. On the left hand side of the drawing, top and bottom, there is some loss where the framing lines have been drawn. 185×162 mm. Dresden, Kupferstichkabinett.
Study for a painting 1635 in Dresden, HdG. 207.
Ben. Vol. I. No. 92. Figure 99. Val. 609. (1635). HdG. 241. (1635).

34

Woman comforts a child, frightened by an inquisitive dog on the door step of a house. About 1636. Pen and bistre; inscribed by a later hand: Rembrant. 184×146 mm. Budapest, Museum of Fine Arts.
Etched by Joseph Schmidt.
Ben. Vol. II. No. 411. Figure 460. HdG. 1387. (Ca. 1635). Val. (Ca. 1636). Rotterdam Catalogue 1956. No. 44a. (Ca. 1635).

35

Sheet of studies. With a woman teaching a child to walk, and a separate study of the child, head and shoulders. About 1646. Pen and bistre. 160×165 mm. Stockholm, National Museum.
Ben. Vol. IV. No. 706. Figure 847. HdG. 1597. (No date). Rotterdam Catalogue. No. 127. (Ca. 1646).

36

Study of a woman, seated on the ground suckling a child. About 1646. Pen and bistre, wash. 175×153 mm.
Stockholm, National Museum.

Ben. Vol. IV. No. 707. Figure 848. HdG. 1595. (No date). Rotterdam Catalogue 1956. No. 63. (1635/40). HB. p. 54. (1635/40).

37

Sheet of sketches. Group of mother and child and neighbour; old woman with spectacles and a large headscarf; the same woman looking up with spectacles in her hand; top right a bearded old man with broad folded headscarf. About 1636. Pen and ink. 178×146 mm. Weimar, Goethe Nationalmuseum.

This old woman occurs again in drawing No. 38. Rembrandt used this type in an etching of 1641, "The Angel ascending from Tobit and his Family." (Bartsch No. 43). and transforms her into the wife of the old Tobit. According to Benesch (Vol. II, No. 301, Fig. 341) this sheet represents: "Three studies of an old woman in a long headress . . . a lost portrait by Rembrandt, known from an etching by A. Riedel, and from an old copy in the museum of Braunschweig – dG. 689 . . . the sitter in that portrait was traditionally called "Rembrandt's Mother."

Ben. Vol. II. No. 301. Figure 341. HdG. 33. (No date).

38

Old Woman with spectacles, reading the Bible. About 1640. Pen and bistre (drawn with a damaged pen). 98×79 mm. Wroclaw, Ossolineum.

This drawing should be grouped together with No. 37. Due to the marked similarity between this and an etching (Bartsch No. 43) it would perhaps be better to date this 1640.

Ben. Vol. II. No. 356. Figure 407. (1637.) HB. p. 26 (much later than 1637).

39

Scribe sharpening his quill by candlelight. About 1635. Pen and wash in bistre. On the right, neck and throat there is some white body colour that has become ineffective. 125×123 mm. Weimar, Großherzogliches Museum.

Ben. Vol. II. No. 336. Figure 288. HdG. 525. (Ca. 1635).

40

Children playing rommelpot, before a half open door. About 1641/42. Pen and bistre wash. A greater part of the drawing has been gone over with a wash in order to tone down outlines and bring the children of the group into the foreground. Inscribed by a later hand: Rembrandt. 212×275 mm. Weimar, Goethe Nationalmuseum.

Ben. Vol. IV. No. 734. Figure 878. HdG. 534. (No date). Val. 784.

41

Three women at the entrance of a house, seen from inside. About 1635. Brush, pen and wash. 250×190 mm. Bayonne, Musee Collection Bonnat.

The drawing shows several corrections. The woman leaning over the door hatch has been drawn in twice; in the second version sketched in broad pen strokes, she is bent forward. Outdoors above the roofs the lightly sketched half profile of a man is effaced by rubbing with the finger.

Ben. Vol. II. No. 406. Figure 462. HdG. 739. (No date). Val. 780. (Ca. 1636).

42

Saskia lying in bed, and a nurse. About 1639. Pen and bistre; certain parts have been rubbed with a finger and the drawing was subsequently framed. 170×134 mm. Weimar, Museum.

Ben. Vol. II. No. 425. Figure 478. HdG. 527. (Ca. 1636). Val. 700. (Ca. 1640).

43

Execution by the sword, in three stages. Also known as: "The Beheading of the Tarquinian Conspirators." About 1640. Pen and bistre. 153×225 mm. London, British Museum.

Benesch takes this as the theme for the "Execution of the Tarquinian Conspirators," and Valentiner as the "Beheading of the Apostle Jacob with his companions looking on." We however see it as the three phases of the execution of a criminal by an executioner. The first phase on the right is closely bound up with the other two. The second stage (second left) can be closely compared with a etching "The Beheading of St. John the Baptist."

(Bartsch No. 92). Rembrandt worked on this execution theme and has presented the 'before-and-after'. The facial characteristics of the criminal are the same in all three cases, but it must be remarked that a cap has been drawn over the hair and eyes in the execution scene.

Ben. Vol. III. No. 479. Figure 600. HdG. 892. Val. 543.

44

Ecce Homo. About 1637. Red chalk. 334×270 mm. Dresden, Kupferstichkabinett.

This drawing bears a marked resemblance to the previous picture. The criminal being led to the execution has been transformed into an "Ecce Homo" presentation. The first part of the group consists of the criminal, the executioner, sympathisers and soldier with lance, on the right other onlookers and in the background further onlookers.

Ben. Vol. I. No. 135. Figure 149. HdG. 221. (Ca. 1630/35). Val. 468. (Ca. 1633).

45

The last supper. After Leonardo da Vinci. About 1635. Signed: Rembrandt f. Red chalk. 365×475 mm. Dresden, Friedrich August II Collection.

According to Benesch this is a drawing "after a Lombard engraving, attributed by Hind to the Master of the Sforza Book of Hours, representing Leonardo da Vinci's fresco in Santa Maria delle Grazie in Milan. The drawing was first laid out in subtle strokes rather as a literal copy after engraving. We consider this first layout to be the work of Rembrandt, and not of a pupil as Valentiner suggested. Rembrandt later modified the drawing with rough chalk strokes giving the figures an angular rhythm. C. Neumann, therefore, dates these modifications in Rembrandt's late period. We do not know of any red chalk drawing by Rembrandt after 1650. The angular rhythm of the modifications finds an analogy in Rembrandt's copies after paintings by Pieter Lastman. The solemn architecture with pilasters, added by Rembrandt, foreshadows the setting of the Supper at Emmaus of 1648 dG. 145. Bredius 578. The moving of the figure group out of the symmetry of the canopy and the architecture is a significant feature in any of Rembrandt's compositions."

Ben. Vol. II. No. 443. Figure 500. Val. 623. (Ca. 1633). HdG. 297. (Ca. 1635).

46

Woman in a rich dress and a fur hat, seen from behind. About 1636. Pen and brush in grey and black. 205×140 mm. Leipzig, Museum of Pictorial Art.

Ben. Vol. II. No. 321. Figure 362. HB. p. 25.

47

Two mummers on horseback. About 1637/38. Pen and bistre, reddish brown washes, touched with yellow and red chalk, some white body colour. 212×154 mm. New York, Pierpont Morgan Library.

Ben. Vol. II. No. 368, Figure 414. Val. 790. (1633/35). HdG. 1109. (No date). Rotterdam Catalogue 1956. No. 74. (1638).

48

Two negro drummers mounted on mules. About 1637/38. Pen and wash in bistre, coloured with red chalk and yellow water colour. 229×171 mm. London, British Museum.

This drawing was begun with a pen and washed with bistre afterwards. Some parts of the garments of the drummer in front and the cover of his drums were filled in with yellow water colour. The red chalk of the collars and parasol was worked into the washed paper whilst it was still wet. The white spaces of the bridle, the drums and the shoes were filled in with red chalk. The face of the drummer in the front seems to be modelled with the brush dipped into some oil colour. Rembrandt made several sketches after a pageant with Africans and mummers which may have taken place in Amsterdam in 1637. J. Q. van Regteren Altena suggests a more definite date, February 1638, when Rembrandt could have observed such groups of Constantin Huygens in the Hague.

Ben. Vol. II. No. 365. Figure 412. Val. 792. (1633/35). HdG. 924. (No date).

49

Quack addressing a crowd at a fair. About 1637. Pen and wash. 188×167 mm. London, Count Antoine Seilern.

Ben. Vol. II. No. 417. Figure 470. Val. 749. (Ca. 1635). HdG. 318. (Ca. 1637).

50

Pastoral. About 1639. Pen and bistre and Indian Ink. 125×123 mm. Wroclaw, Ossolineum.

We feel that a comic theatre scene must have inspired this drawing, since the herdsman is holding his instrument so unprofessionally and the shepherdess is looking at him so sceptically. Rembrandt would naturally have known exactly how such an instrument should be played (compare No. 82).

51

Man transformed into angel and frightened elderly couple. Also known as "Manoah's Offering" (Judges XIII v. 19–20). About 1639. Pen and bistre in reddish brown. (The head at the bottom is by a strange hand and shows through from the back of the drawing.) 175×190 mm. Berlin, Kupferstichkabinett.

For the secondary character of the drawing see the text on page 45.

Ben. Vol. I. No. 180. Figure 193. Val. 134. (Ca. 1637). HdG. 31. (Ca. 1635/40).

52

Hagar and Ishmael with the angel in the desert. (Genesis 21 v. 14–17.) About 1640/42. Pen and bistre, wash. 170×175 mm. Hamburg, Kunsthalle. (Inv. 21946).

Falck regards the present drawing as a copy by Phillips Koninck after Rembrandt. Gerson correctly rejects this attribution to Koninck but undervalues the drawing in giving it to the Rembrandt school, Comparison with other drawings proves conclusively that it is firmly rooted in Rembrandt's development.

Ben. Vol. III. No. 498. Figure 621. Val. 31. (Ca. 1638).

53

Susanna at the bath and the two elders. (Apocypha, The History of Susanna, v. 19–21). About 1641/44. Pen and bistre, over traces of metal point; the upper corners slanted, inscribed by a later hand: Rebrandt. 197×170 mm. Dresden, Kupferstichkabinett.

This drawing has been the subject of much discussion. It was first published by Burchard, who raised some objection to the landscape prepared with a metal point, which he attributed to another hand, but who accepted the figure composition, comparing it with the "Portrait of Jan Cornelisz Sylvius, Ben. No. 763. He saw in it the preparatory sketch for a lost painting preserved in a drawn copy in the Museum at Budapest. Kauffmann in his first essay rejected the present drawing. In his second essay in which he proved that the Budapest drawing renders a previous stage of the painting in Berlin of 1647 (dG. 55. Bredius 516), corresponding with the present drawing in so far as in both works the Elder close to Susanna seizes her with his left arm, he accepted it. Kauffmann dated the present drawing and consequently also the supposed first version of the Berlin painting about 1635, presuming that Rembrandt reworked it as late as 1647. Valentiner rejected the present drawing. Kauffmann's early dating of the present drawing and of the Berlin painting is untenable. The style of the drawing points clearly to the period of 1641/44. The painting shows no traces which could be attributed to the 1630's. For the present drawing and the painting finally resulting from it, however, Rembrandt made use of the series of drawings done about 1637 in connection with the painting (dG. 57. Bredius 505).

Ben. Vol. III. No. 536. Figure 666. Val. 260 (a later copy). HB. p. 52/53 (copy).

54

Samson and Delilah, before the betrayal. (Judges 16, v. 18–19). About 1642/43. Pen and bistre wash. The two warriors covered with white. 181×227 mm. Groningen, Museum. (Inv. 197). C. Hofstede de Groot bequest.

Ben. Vol. III. No. 530. Figure 659. Val. 142. Ca. 1634. Rotterdam Catalogue 1956. No. 79. (1635/38).

55

Christ and the woman taken in adultery. About 1641/44. Pen and bistre; the arch of the door above Christ has been erased with white. Left hand bottom corner a free hand frame line by Rembrandt. 240×183 mm. Dresden, Kupferstichkabinett.

This is one of the few composition drawings by Rembrandt. The construction, the distribution of the figures and the accentuation of the same were merely an exercise in drawing. All the detail has been neglected to such an extent that the theme is only recognisable, when compared with others works.

Ben. Vol. III. No. 534. Figure 663. HdG. 216 (Early period). HB. p. 52/53 (Copy).

56

Landscape with two men, fishing in a bay, and a village on the opposite embankment. About 1640/41. Pen and bistre. 110×172 mm. Wroclaw, Ossolineum.

Ben. Vol. IV. No. 798. Figure 942.

57

An estate amidst the trees, on the Amstel river. About 1640/41. Pen and bistre. 105×195 mm. Dresden, Kupferstichkabinett.

On the reverse the authentic signature.

Ben. Vol. IV. No. 943. HdG. 285. (Ca. 1641).

58

Farm house amidst trees. About 1641. Pen and bistre; inscribed by a later hand: Rembrandt van Ryn. 183×326 mm. Dresden, Kupferstichkabinett.

The figures and the terrain in the foreground are broadly drawn with a reed pen in a manner which is also found in figure compositions of the early 1640's. Rembrandt made use of such strongly drawn lines in the terrain to push the main subject back into space.

Ben. Vol. VI. No. 801. Figure 948. HdG. 286. (Ca. 1641).

59

A canal between bushes, with a windmill in the distance. About 1645. Black chalk. 159×116 mm. Wroclaw, Ossolineum.

Ben. Vol. IV. No. 817. Figure 957.

60

Pastures with a windmill, outside a town. About 1641. Pen and wash. 142×288 mm. Chantilly, Musée Conde.

Ben. Vol. IV. No. 802. Figure 949. HdG. 575. (No date).

61

Cottages before a stormy sky, in sunlight. About 1641. Pen washes in bistre and Indian ink, upper left corner restored. 182×245 mm. Vienna, Albertina.

Ben. Vol. IV. No. 800. Figure 947. HdG. 1484. (No date). Rotterdam Catalogue 1956. No. 117. (1640/42).

62

Landscape with a bridge, in the middle distance. About 1640/41. Pen and bistre, some washes. 115×159 mm. Wroclaw, Ossolineum.

Ben. Vol. IV. No. 793. Figure 941.

63

Star of the Kings. About 1641/42. Pen and bistre, wash; a figure in the right portion obliterated with wash. Signed: Rembrandt f. 204×323 mm. London, British Museum.

Ben. Vol. IV. No. 736. Figure 882. Val. 783. (1636). HdG. 1129. (Ca. 1635).

64

Beggar playing the violin, walking with his wife and a dog, two children to the right with hoop. About 1642/43. Pen and bistre; the paper is damaged on the right but restored. 129×93 mm. Warsaw, University Library (Stanislaus Potocki Collection) (T. 1155, N. 15).

Ben. Vol. IV. No. 739. Figure 883.

65

Sheet of studies, group of orientals in the street, and two half length studies of the same beggar on either side. About 1641/42. Pen and bistre wash. 143×182 mm. Warsaw, University Library (Stanislaus Potocki Collection T. 1155, N. 9).

Ben. Vol. IV. No. 667. Figure 806.

66

The dismissal of Hagar and Ishmael. (Genesis 21. v. 10—14). About 1642/43. Pen and wash in bistre, slightly heightened with white; the figure of Abraham has been inserted on another piece of paper. 185×236 mm. London, British Museum.

The heavily undulating lines approach closely "The Mourners beneath the Cross," No. 520 Ben. Rembrandt treated the Hagar subject frequently. See No. 52. "The Angel appearing to Hagar and Ishmael in the Wilderness." A drawing in the Louvre, Lugt 1208, shows a similar figure group with slight changes. Ben. Vol. III. No. 524. Figure 652. Val. 20. (Ca. 1637). HdG. 865. (Ca. 1637).

67

Abraham and Sarah after the dismissal of Hagar. Also known as "Tobit reading to Anna from the Bible." About 1640/41. Pen and bistre. 135×195 mm. Constance, Wessenberg Gallery.

See Text page 50.

Ben. Vol. III. No. 489, Figure 611. (1640/41).

68

The carpenter's workshop. Or "The Holy Family in the Carpenter's Workshop." About 1640/42. Pen and bistre, washes in bistre and Indian Ink. 184×246 mm. London, British Museum.

Ben. Vol. III. No. 516. Figure 643. Val. 325 A. (Ca. 1640).

69

The carpenter's workshop, or "The Holy Family in the Carpenter's Workshop." About 1640/42. Pen and wash with bistre and Indian ink; inscribed by a later hand: Rembrandt. 156×215 mm. Paris, Louvre (Prints Dept).

Ben. Vol. III. No. 517. Figure 642.

70

Christ awakening the apostles on the Mount of Olives. About 1641/42. Pen and bistre, wash; inscribed: 115 Rijn. 168×208 mm. Hanover, Dr. Bernhard Sprengel.

Ben. Vol. III. No. 513. Figure 638. Val. 447. (Ca. 1638). HdG. 1504. (No date).

71

The good samaritan arriving at the inn. About 1641/43. Pen and bistre, wash, some corrections with white. 184×287 mm. London, British Museum.

Ben. Vol. III. No. 518 A. Figure 646. Val. 379. (Ca. 1648). HdG. 885. (Ca. 1648).

72

Tobias, frightened by the fish, with the angel. In a mountainous landscape. (Apocrypha, Tobit, 6. v. 2—3). About 1644. Pen and bistre, wash, heightened with white. As Rosenberg points out, a small strip of paper has been cut out. The lowest portion of 20 mm. has been pasted on again by the artist himself, and does not fit the upper part. 205×273 mm. Berlin, Kupferstichkabinett.

Benesch does not agree with the doubts expressed by Valentiner and Lugt about the present drawing, all the more as he accepts some of the works quoted by Lugt as material for comparison, as significant works of the 1640's.

Ben. Vol. III. No. 559. Figure 689. Val. 235. (Ca. 1645). HdG. 40. (No date).

73

Tobias with the angel disembowelling the fish. In an open landscape. (Apocrypha, Tobit, 6. v. 3—5). About 1640/42. Pen and bistre, corrected with white body colour. 166×278 mm. Wroclaw, Ossolineum.

Ben. Vol. III. No. 497. Figure 620.

74

The angel showing Tobias the fish. (Apocrypha, Tobit, 6. v. 3—5). About 1649/50. Pen and bistre, wash; Tobias's right arm corrected with white body colour. 167×161 mm. Dresden, Kupferstichkabinett.

Compare the style of this with Nos. 72 and 73.

Ben. Vol. III. No. 636. Figure 771. Val. 207. (1636). HdG. 207. (Ca. 1654).

75

Tobit and Anna with the goat. (Apocrypha, Tobit, 2. v. 12—14). About 1645. Pen and bistre. The head of Anna seems to have been drawn twice, first more erect and facing front. 146×185 mm. Berlin, Kupfer-stichkabinett.

This drawing is connected with the painting of 1645, Berlin, Kaiser Friedrich Museum. dG. 64. Bredius 514. J. Rosenberg and Valentiner consider this drawing to be later than the painting, dating it about 1650. Benesch is inclined to follow Hofstede de Groot's and Lilienfeld's dating to about 1645. The present drawing is more advanced in style; it corresponds much more to the actual style of the painting.

Ben. Vol. III. No. 572. Figure 704. Val. 223. (Ca. 1650). HdG. 38. (Ca. 1645).

76

The return of the prodigal son. (Luke 15. v. 18—20). About 1642. Pen and wash in bistre, corrections with white body colour. 190×227 mm. Haarlem, Museum Teyler.

The main group, also the boy at the left and the balustrade on which he is resting are by Rembrandt; the washes and the architectural setting of the background are by another hand. The drawing has generally been dated about 1635/36, because Rembrandt etched the same subject in 1636, B. 91 Hind, Etchings 147. There is however no connection in style between the two compositions. Note the vigorous modelling of the figures and the strong outlines.

Ben. Vol. III. No. 519. Figures 641. Val. 388. (1636). HdG. 1318. (Ca. 1635). Rotterdam Catalogue 1956. No. 108. (1640/45).

77

The Carpenter's Workshop. Also known as "The Holy Family in the Carpenter's Workshop." About 1648/49. Pen and bistre. 173×227 mm. Rotterdam, Museum Boymans.

Ben. Vol. III. No. 620. Figure 750. Val. 328. (Ca. 1645). HdG. 1347. (No date).

78

Seated girl, in a large head cloth, full-length, and another sketch of her head and shoulders. Pen and bistre. 110×122 mm. Dresden, Kupferstichkabinett.

Ben. Vol. IV. No. 657. Figure 796. (Ca. 1640/42). HdG. 258. (No date). We put this at a much later date, 1652.

79

Vertumnus and Pomona. (Ovid. Metamorphosis, XIV p. 654—697). About 1642/44. Pen and bistre, wash. 177×218 mm. Amsterdam, Kupferstichkabinett (Formerly J. Qu. Van Regteren Altena, Amsterdam).

Ben. Vol. III. No. 553. Figure 683. Val. 613. (Ca. 1638). Rotterdam Catalogue 1956. No. 107. (1641/44). HB. p. 52 (1638 or earlier).

80

Satan showing Christ the kingdoms of the world. (Matthew 4, v. 8—9). About 1649. Pen and bistre, wash, in some places covered with white. The step like shape under Satan's left foot was scrawled in by another hand. 232×199 mm. Berlin, Kupferstichkabinett.

A double circle is drawn around the two figures which, according to Valentiner, indicates that the drawing was a design for a plate or metal platter like those made for Jan Lutma, or a piece of Delft fayence.

Ben. Vol. III. No. 635. Figure 770. Val. 356. (Ca. 1645). HdG. 54. (No date).

81

The skeleton rider. A human skeleton mounted on a skeleton of a horse. About 1649. Pen and bistre. 153×148. Darmstadt, Hessisches Landesmuseum.

Ben. Vol. IV. No. 728. Figure 871. Rotterdam Catalogue 1956. No. 225. (1653/56). HB. p. 55. (Middle of the 50th year).

82

A pastoral scene. About 1646/47. Pen and bistre, parts altered with covering; the composition is arched above. 200×180 mm. E. R. Johnson, Camden, New Jersey, U.S.A.

Ben. Vol. IV. No. 748. Figure 891. Val. 617. (Ca. 1642).

83

Mercury, Argus and Io. About 1648/50. Pen and bistre. 176×263 mm. Warsaw, University Library.

Zeus fell in love with the priestess, Io. Hera, for this reason, changed Io into a white cow, and appointed the three hundred eyed giant Argus to watch over her. Zeus sent Mercury to Argus and with the aid of his magic staff he caused, one by one, the eyes of the watchman to close in sleep and then killed him.

A drawing in the possession of Ch. Albert de Burlet, Basle employs almost the same compostition, but with slight variations in the poses of Argus and Mercury. It is apparently a pupil's variation (183×264 mm) of the master's work.

Ben. Vol. III. No. 627. Figure 763.

84

The daughters of Cecrops, opening the chest containing the little Erichthonius. About 1648/49. Pen and bistre, corrected with white body colour which has since become oxydised. 117×218 mm. Groningen, Museum.

The goddess Athene gave the daughters of the King Cecrops a basket which contained the little Erichthonius, half man and half snake. Athene forbade anyone to open the basket. The sisters ignored this command and on seeing the young Erichthonius became mad. Auglauros, who is kneeling at the left, has lifted the lid of the basket, which has been drawn twice, the earlier version being covered with white. Pandrosos and Herse stand by in attitudes of alarm.

85

Old man seated, in front of his bed, having his feet bathed; a woman is pouring water from a jug by the chimney place at the left. (Interpretation of the scene unknown.) About 1649/50. Pen and wash in bistre, inscribed: Rembrandt. 170×234 mm. Warsaw, University Library (Royal Collection T.174, N.313).

Benesch entitles this picture "Old Tobit seated."

Another proposed meaning, that Odysseus returns as an unknown beggar and is recognised by a scar when having his feet bathed (Odyssey XIX 386) is untenable. Rembrandt would certainly have found some way of expressing this in his drawing.

In a copy, the fireplace and the woman pouring water from the jug in front of it are omitted. Falck according to Valentiner, considers the present drawing also a copy, the linear structure of the delicate work, however, is so sensitive that it can hardly be attributed to an imitator.

Ben. Vol. III. No. 644. Figure 784. Rotterdam Catalogue 1956. No. 130. (1645/50).

86

Christ awakening the Apostles on the Mount of Olives. About 1648/49. Pen and wash in bistre. 165×260 mm. Warsaw, University Library.

Ben. Vol. III. No. 613. Figure 745. Val. 448. (Ca. 1645).

87

A man of Gibeah offers hospitality to the Levite and his Concubine. (Judges XIX. v. 17–20.) About 1644. (With some later additions). Pen and wash in brown and dark brown bistre. 180×246 mm. London, British Museum.

Hind assumes that the upper part of the body of the woman and the head of the mule and the head of the old man of Gibeah were reworked by Rembrandt in darker ink. It may be added that the cap of the Prophet was also redrawn in the same darker ink.

The reworkings in darker ink were correctly observed by Hind and may perhaps indicate that Rembrandt went over his own drawing several years later before he dealt with the subject anew.

Ben. Vol. III. No. 554. Figure 684. Val. 340. (Ca. 1645). HdG. 881. (Ca. 1645). HB. p. 52.

88

Elijah and the prophets of Baal. (1 Kings XVIII. 22–39). About 1647. Pen and wash, bistre. 204×315 mm. Constance, Wessenberg Gallery.

The present drawing shows one of the most magnificent inventions of Rembrandt foreshadowing one of his latest etchings, dated 1659, St. Peter and St. John at the Gate of the Temple. B. 94. Hind, Etchings 301. Ben. Vol. III. No. 593. Figure 724.

89

The bretheren of Joseph requesting Benjamin from their father. (Genesis 42. v. 29–36). About 1643. Pen and bistre; the man on the left seated on the step has been superimposed by Rembrandt. 176×231 mm. Amsterdam, Rijksprentenkabinet.

Hofstede de Groot and Lilienfeld interpreted the subject as indicated above. P. Buberl (Wickhoff Seminarstudien), Lugt and Henkel see in it the report of the bretheren to their father after their return from the second journey to Egypt (Genesis 45. v. 25–26) because Benjamin holds in his hand Joseph's cup. To the latter opinion it may be objected that according to the Bible, Joseph gave to Benjamin 300 pieces of silver and five raiments of garment, but not the cup. Furthermore, the psychological note is more that of hesitation, deliberation and persuasion than that of excited report of extraordinary happenings. Hofstede de Groot's opinion is then more likely than the latter. Ben. Vol. III. No. 541. Figure 671. Val. 117. (Ca. 1638). HdG. 1160. (No date). Rotterdam Catalogue 1956. No. 90. (1638/40).

90

A blind beggar, guided by a little boy who receives alms from an old man. About 1647/48. Pen and bistre. 168×194 mm. Vienna, Albertina.
Ben. Vol. IV. No. 750. Figure 898. HdG. 1451. (No date). Rotterdam Catalogue 1956. No. 94. (1639/40).

91

The parable of the unworthy wedding guest. (Matthew 22. v. 8–14). About 1648/49. Pen and wash. 183×265 mm. Vienna, Albertina.
Etched by Johann Daniel Laurentz, 1756, and by Adam Bartsch.
Ben. Vol. III. No. 612. Figure 742. HdG. 1419. (No date). Rotterdam Catalogue 1956. No. 137. (1648/49).

92

The parable of the labourers in the vineyard. (Matthew 20. v. 1–16). About 1648/49. Pen and bistre; the turban of the master of the vineyard is drawn by a later hand on a superimposed piece of paper. 185×272 mm. Rotterdam, Museum Boymans.

On the verso is a sketch of the figure of the master which shows through the paper. This drawing has been reworked extensively, by a later hand, which led Valentiner to doubt it. The original pen work is in an olive bistre tone, from which the reddish brown tone of the reworkings differs visibly.
The following parts are reworkings: the horizontal steps in the lower left portion; the estrade on which the parapet is placed (it cuts off the figure of the master at its base); the turban of the master; the flourish in the empty space right of centre.
Ben. Vol. III. No. 604. Figure 735. Val. 370. (Ca. 1655). HdG. 1349. (No date).

93

The parable of the labourers in the vineyard. (Matthew 20. v. 1–16). About 1648/50. Pen and dark olive greyish brown bistre, slight washes in brown bistre, reworkings by a later hand: table cloth, zig-zag hatchings and greyish-black pen strokes in the background, grey washes; inscribed by a later hand: Rembrandt. 152×195 mm. New York, The Pierpont Morgan Library.
Ben. Vol. III. No. 605. Figure 736. Val. 369. (Ca. 1650). HdG. 1082. (No date).

94

The parable of the talents. (Matthew 25. v. 14–30). About 1652. Reed pen and bistre, erased in some parts by a finger. 173×218 mm. Paris, Louvre, L. Bonnat bequest.
A copy is in Hamburg. The geometrical articulation of the figures here is specially clear.
Ben. Vol. V. No. 910. Figure 1120. Val. 364. (1652). HdG. 694. (No date).

95

Man dictating and scribe. About 1648. Pen and bistre. 145×145 mm. Paris, Louvre, Department of prints.
Ben. Vol. III. No. 599. Figure 730. HdG. 642. (No date). Rotterdam Catalogue 1956. No. 136. (Ca. 1650).

96

The eastern gate at Rhenen. (Oostpoort or Bergpoort). About 1647/49. Pen and bistre, wash, inscribed by a
later hand: Rimbrand. 130×235 mm. Bayonne, Musée, Collection Bonnat.
Photograph: Caisse nationale des monuments historiques.
Ben. Vol. IV. No. 827. Figure 974. HdG. 761. (No date).

97

A coach. About 1649. Pen and wash in bistre; arched above; the paper has been cut and joined down the
centre. 194×254 mm. London, British Museum.
Ben. Vol. IV. No. 756. Figure 901. HdG. 966. (No date). HB. p. 55. (middle of 50th year).

98

A winter landscape, with a hamlet; a man repairing a sailing boat in the foreground. About 1648/50. Pen and
bistre, washes in bistre and Indian ink. Grey wash, bottom left by another hand. Inscribed by a later hand:
Rembrand. 103×180 mm. Amsterdam, Rijksprentenkabinet, C. Hofstede de Groot bequest.
Ben. Vol. IV. No. 837. Figure 981. HdG. 1309. (No date). Rotterdam Catalogue 1956. No. 144. (Ca. 1646).

99

View of Diemen, seen from the Diemerdijk. About 1649/50. Pen and bistre, wash, on brownish paper.
90×170 mm. Haarlem, Museum Teyler.
Ben. Vol. VI. No. 1229. Figure 1455. HdG. 1333. (No date). Rotterdam Catalogue 1956. No. 163. (1647/52).

100

Farm Houses at the Amsteldijk, in Summer. About 1650. Pen and bistre, wash, on yellowish paper. Subsequently the dike, the railings, the rider on the left hand side, the land line on the right were filled in to
round off the drawing. The frame line is by another hand. 143×207 mm. Dresden, Kupferstichkabinett.
Ben. Vol. VI. No. 1234. Figure 1461. HdG. 284. (Ca. 1650).

101

Farm Houses at the Amsteldijk, in Winter. About 1650. Pen and bistre, slightly washed; inscribed by a later
hand: Rembrant. 102×188 mm. Paris, Louvre, Walter Gay bequest (Inv. 29027).
Ben. Vol. VI. No. 1235. Figure 1462.

102

The bend of the Amstel river near Kostverloren in Autumn or Winter. About 1651/52. Pen and bistre, wash,
some white body colour. 97×199 mm. Chatsworth Settlement, Devonshire Collection, Derbyshire.
Ben. Vol. VI. No. 1268. Figure 1495. HdG. 839. (No date).

103

View of Houtwaal, a little village near Amsterdam. About 1651. Pen and bistre, wash, some white body colour,
the reed and the fence tinged with a greyish tone. 125×182 mm. Chatsworth Settlement, (Inv 1032)
Devonshire Collection, Derbyshire.
Ben. Vol. VI. No. 1261. Figure 1483. HdG. 846. (No date).

104

The Omval between Amstel and Diemermeer. About 1653. Pen and bistre, wash. 108×187 mm. Constance,
Wessenberg Gallery.
Ben. Vol. VI. No. 1322. Figure 1557. HdG. 196. (No date).

105

Farm Houses beneath the trees in Winter time. About 1653/54. Reed pen and bistre, on light brown prepared

paper; inscription "Rembrant" erased and replaced by "Jan Van Goyen." 131×230 mm. Leningrad, Hermitage (Inv. 5327).
Ben. Vol. VI. No. 1328. Figure 1562. HdG. 1530. (No date).

106

An avenue of trees leading into the distance; on the left a woman with a child. About 1654/55. Reed pen and wash in bistre; the paper right and left at the top has been toned or dirtied. The stroke across the sky, left is not part of the drawing. 99×235 mm. Berlin, Kupferstichkabinett.
Ben. Vol. VI. No. 1341. Figure 1575. HdG. 177. (No date).

107

Thatched cottage with a tree and a man walking at the right. About 1652. Pen and ink and bistre. 101×176 mm. Berlin, Kupferstichkabinett.
Ben. Vol. VI. No. 1283. Figure 1511.

108

Farm building at the dijk. About 1648. Pen and bistre; washes in bistre and Indian ink. Inscribed by another hand: Rembrant. 143×242 mm. London, British Museum.
Ben. Vol. IV. No. 832. Figure 985. (Ca. 1648). HdG. 950. (No date).

109

Landscape with a drawbridge and a cottage at the right. About 1648/50. Pen and wash in bistre; inscribed by a later hand: Rembrandt. 156×268 mm. Vienna, Albertina.
Etched by Johann Daniel Laurentz, 1756. Gersaint 402.
Ben. Vol. IV. No. 851. Figure 999. HdG. 1487. (No date).

110

Harvesters resting in a field. About 1649/50. Pen, over some traces of black chalk. 176×250 mm. Paris, Bibliotheque Nationale.
We do not incline to the opinion expressed by W. Drost, in "Elsheimer als Zeichner," (Stuttgart 1957) that Rembrandt used this, and many other of Elsheimer's drawings as a basis for his own.
Ben. Vol. III. No. 640. Figure 775. (Ca. 1649/50).

111

A village street with three cows, and a rider accompanied by dogs, approaching from the right. About 1647/48. Pen and bistre, wash. 195×265 mm. Berlin, Heirs of Rathenau (formerly).
Ben. Vol. IV. No. 752. Figure 899.

112

Woody landscape with a horseman. About 1648/50. Pen and bistre, wash. 167×230 mm. Leningrad, Hermitage
Ben. Vol. IV. No. 852. Figure 998. HdG. 1534. (No date).

113

A clump of trees and a farm house by a road, leading into the distance. About 1648/50. Pen, brush and wash in bistre; reworked in the leafage by another hand; inscribed by a later hand; Rembrandt. f. 175×335 mm. Leningrad, Hermitage.
Ben. Vol. IV. No. 850. Figure 1001.

114

Riverscape with a sailing boat, and a town in the distance. About 1654/55. Reed pen, brush, wash and bistre. 109×213 mm. New York, Edwin A. Seasongood.
Ben. Vol. VI. No. 1349. Figure 1583.

115

'Het Molentje' seen from the Amsteldijk. About 1654/55. Pen and bistre, wash; at the right a slip of paper 26 mm. wide is joined to the main sheet. 93×214 mm. Vienna, Albertina.
Ben. Vol. VI. No. 1354. Figure 1588. HdG. 1494. (No date). Rotterdam Catalogue 1956. No. 195. (1654/55). 87

116

Riverscape with boats. About 1650. Pen, brush and wash in bistre; inscribed on the reverse: Rembrandt f.; at the right a strip of paper, ca. 13 mm. was added to the main sheet; it was originally empty but has since been filled in by another hand. 116×186 mm. Warsaw, University Library, Count S. Potocki Collection (174 No. 316).
Ben. Vol. VI. Add. No. 18. Figure 1727. (Ca. 1650). Rotterdam Catalogue 1956. No. 199a. (1650/56).

117

Portrait of a scholar at this writing table, supposedly the writing master lieven Willemsz Van Coppenool. About 1646. Pen and wash in bistre, erased many times with the finger, frame line top and bottom by Rembrandt, cut left and right. 161×150 mm. Budapest, Museum of Fine Arts.
Ben. Vol. IV. No. 766. Figure 908. Val. 742. (Ca. 1658). HdG. 1373. (No date). Rotterdam Catalogue 1956. No. 233a (before 1658). HB. p. 56. (Ca. 1658).

118

Old jew in high hat standing with his left arm extended, in profile to right, three quarter length. About 1651. Pen and bistre wash. 95×71 mm. Budapest, Museum of Fine Arts.
Ben. Vol. V. No. 1078. Figure 1295. (Ca. 1651). HdG. 1375. (No date).

119

Seated old man with a stock, half length. 1650. Pen and bistre; the right hand resting on the stick or the armrest of the chair; this has been carefully erased with white body colour. 130×110 mm. Dresden, Kupferstichkabinett.
On the reverse, the date 1650. The drawing is very similar to a painting by Rembrandt of a bearded old man in the Dresden Gallery.
Ben. Vol. V. No. 1069. Figure 1287. HdG. 245. (Date cannot be conclusively confirmed).

120

Two men in discussion; one in high cap facing front, the other in profile to the left. About 1657/58. Pen and bistre, wash. 118×70 mm. Budapest, Museum of Fine Arts.
On the reverse, inscription by a 17th Century hand: troonyen. en. posttueren . . . van den ouden . . . tot.
Ben. Vol. 1134. Figure 1355. HdG. 1382. (No date).

121

A woman hanging on the gallows. About 1645/46. Pen and bistre, wash; the upper corners slanted. 176×93 mm. New York, Metropolitan Museum of Art (Inv. 76437).
Ben. Vol. V. No. 1105. Figure 1324.

122

Two old shepherds. About 1655. Pen and bistre. 150×128 mm. Budapest, Museum of Fine Arts.
Ben. Vol. V. No. 1087. Figure 1307. HdG. 1376. (No date).

123

Gentleman in a large hat seated by a window, reading. About 1655/56. Pen and bistre, wash. 181×171 mm. Munich, Graphische Sammlung.
Ben. Vol. V. No. 1173. Figure 1400. Val. 735. (Ca. 1647). HdG. 419. (Ca. 1646). HB. p. 87 (doubtful if by Rembrandt).

124

Rembrandt's studio. About 1655/56. Pen and Indian ink, wash, touched with white body colour (partly oxidised). 205×190 mm. Oxford, Ashmolean Museum.
Ben. Vol. V. No. 1161. Figure 1383. HdG. 1136. (No date).

124a

Rembrandt teaching, with pupils working at a female model. Attributed to Samuel van Hoogstraten. Pen and bistre. 182×317 mm. Weimar, Museum.
Samuel van Hoogstraten (1627–1678) was a pupil of Rembrandt's with Carel Fabricius and Abraham Funerius.

125a

Teacher correcting drawing during live drawing class. Attributed to Rembrandt's pupil Constantin van Renesse. Black and white chalk, brown wash. 180×266 mm. Darmstadt, Hessisches Landesmuseum.

Constantin van Renesse was a pupil of Rembrandt's around 1649.

A comparison of the two student's drawings on the same theme, indicates that either one of the drawings was inspired by the other, or that both were inspired by a third. The Weimar drawing would appear to us to be the earlier since here, the master bears a resemblance to Rembrandt and is shown, not drawing, but correcting verbally. Worthy of note also is the fact that the ink bottle in the girdle of the student on the left of the Weimar drawing has been changed to a dagger (!) in the Darmstadt drawing.

125

Female nude standing, with her left arm raised. About 1654/56. Pen and bistre, wash, on brownish paper. 270×140 mm. Amsterdam, Rijkprentenkabinet.

Ben. Vol. V. No. 1118. Figure 1340. HdG. 1199. (No date). HB. p. 87.

126

Nude figure of a girl reclining. About 1654/56. Pen and bistre, wash on parchment. 175×255 mm. Oxford, Library of Christ Church.

Ben. Vol. V. No. 1115. Figure 1333. Rotterdam Catalogue 1956. No. 243. (1658/61). HB. p. 87. (By another hand).

127

Female nude with her head bent forward, asleep. About 1657/58. Pen and brush in bistre, wash, some oxidised. white. 135×283 mm. Amsterdam, Rijksprentenkabinet.

Ben. Vol. V. No. 1137. Figure 1351. HdG. 1032. (Ca. 1650/55). Rotterdam Catalogue 1956. No. 241. (1658).

128

Female nude seated on a chair, seen from behind. About 1654/56. Pen and brush in bistre, on brownish paper. 222×185 mm. Munich, Graphische Sammlung.

Ben. Vol. V. No. 1107. Figure 1326. HdG. 502 (1661 genuine?). Rotterdam Catalogue 1956. No. 240. (1658/60). HB. p. 87.

129

Young girl, half nude, resting on a cushion. About 1654/56. Pen and brush in bistre, with erased highlights, on brownish paper. On the face, the back and the cushion the paper surface has been damaged by some unidentifiable means. 142×175 mm. Dresden, Kupferstichkabinett.

On the reverse a contemporary inscription in Latin.

Ben. Vol. V. No. 1109. Figure 1332. HdG. 254. (No date). HB. p. 87. (possible copy).

130

Boy drawing at a desk, probably Titus. About 1655/56. Pen and bistre and brush, rubbed with the finger. In the hair and the hat the paper has sustained some damage. The paper has been cut from left to right with some loss to the paper. 182×140 mm. Dresden, Kupferstichkabinett.

Ben. Vol. V. No. 1195. Figure 1314. Val. 716. (Ca. 1655). HdG. 244. (Ca. 1655).

131

Self portrait in studio attire, full length. About 1655/56. Pen and bistre, on brownish paper. 203×134 mm. Amsterdam, Rembrandt Huis.

The present drawing is one of the most magnificent and human documents of self revelation. It is linked with an entire group of portrait and figure studies, done about 1655/56, which are among Rembrandt's most brilliant creations. Inscribed by a collector of the eighteenth century, (translated): "Rembrandt van Rijn drawn by himself, as he appeared in his studio."

Ben. Vol. V. No. 1171. Figure 1393. Val. 665. (Ca. 1654). HdG. 994. (Ca. 1654).

132

Young man in a high crowned hat, (Titus?) resting against two pillows on a low chair, asleep. About 1655/56. Pen   89

and wash in bistre. Benesch says: "All the brushwork in reddish brown, mainly in the pillow and chair, is not by Rembrandt." 161×178 mm. London, British Museum.
Ben. Vol. V. No. 1092. Figure 1311. HdG. 903. (Ca. 1655).

133
Boy in a wide brimmed hat, resting his chin on his hand. About 1655/56. Pen and bistre, wash. 85×90 mm. London, British Museum.
Ben. Vol. V. No. 1093. Figure 1312. Val. 715. (1655). HdG. 905. (Ca. 1655).

134
Young girl looking out of a window. 1650/51. Reed pen and bistre; slightly washed in light blue by an alien hand, some white body colour. 97×107 mm. Dresden, Kupferstichkabinett.
The same model is represented in the painting "The Young Girl with a Broom," Washington, National Gallery, dG. 299, Bredius 378. The painting as executed differs slightly from the drawing particularly in the pose of the left hand. This form of the half figure resting on a door or window was initiated by Rembrandt and was taken up with great enthusiasm by his pupils and subsequently other followers.
Ben Vol. V. No. 1170. Figure 1394. Val. 708 (1651). HdG. 253 (Ca. 1651).

135
Girl leaning on a door, (Apparently Hendrickje). About 1655/56. Brush and wash in bistre, some white body colour. 165×125 mm. Stockholm, Nationalmuseum.
Ben. Vol. V. No. 1102. Figure 1320. Val. 712. (Ca. 1657). HdG. 1591. (No date). Rotterdam Catalogue 1956. No. 231. (No date).

136
Young girl asleep, resting her head on her right hand. About 1655/56. Pen and brush in bistre. On the right cheek and left ear, the remains of white body colour. The face and under the right arm have been washed apparently a bit too late to dissolve the colour. 144×115 mm. Dresden, Kupferstichkabinett.
Ben. Vol. V. No. 1100. Figure 1319. Val. 710. (Ca. 1657). HdG. 256. (No date).

137
Female nude reclining on cushions to the left with her right arm raised as if grasping a rope, and looking at the spectator. About 1654/56. Pen and bistre, wash. 233×178 mm. Chicago, The Art Institute of Chicago.
Ben. Vol. V. No. 1127. Figure 1348. Rotterdam Catalogue 1956. No. 235. (Ca. 1658/60). HB. p. 87.

138
Study of a female nude standing by a chair with her left arm raised, supported by a sling. About 1661. Pen and wash in bistre, some covering white surrounding the outlines; the paper along the left outline cut out. 276×135 mm. London, British Museum.
Ben. Vol. V. No. 1145. Figure 1369. HdG. 938. (Ca. 1660).

139
Female nude, in a long veil, seated on a chair before a curtain. About 1661. Pen and wash in bistre, touches of red and white chalk and body white. 287×193 mm. Rotterdam, F. Koenigs Collection (Inv. R. 20).
The same model with a personable facial expression also occurs in the "Costume Study" in the British Museum (Ben. Vol. VI. No. 1174. Figure 1396). We believe, that we also see this type of woman in the figure of the angel with whom Jacob wrestled the night. (Painting of ca. 1659/60, Dahlem Museum, Berlin).
Ben. Vol. V. No. 1144. Figure 1368. HdG. 1033. (Ca. 1635/40). Rotterdam Catalogue 1956. No. 242. (Ca. 1661).

140
Abraham's sacrifice. About 1650. Pen and bistre; the upper corners rounded. 180×155 mm. Dresden. Kupferstichkabinett.
On the reverse: Sketch of an old man's head bent forward in profile to the right. Pen.
Ben. Vol. V. No. 863. Figure 1067. Val. 50. (Ca. 1655 genuine?). HdG. 198. (No date).

141

Judith beheading Holofernes. (Apocrypha. Judith 13). About 1657. Pen and bistre. 182×150 mm. Naples, Pinacoteca.

Ben. Vol. V. No. 897. Figure 1108. Val. 214. (Ca. 1655). HdG. 1144. (No date).

142

Joseph expounding the prisoner's dreams. (Genesis 40. v. 9—19). About 1652. Reed pen and bistre. 157×189 mm. Amsterdam, Rijksprentenkabinet.

Ben. Vol. V. No. 912. Figure 1122. Val. 110. (Ca. 1652). HdG. 1159. (No date).

143

Christ consoled by the angel, on the Mount of Olives. About 1652. Reed pen and bistre. White body colour in Christ's eyes. Framing top right and left were hastily drawn in by Rembrandt. Dresden, Kupferstich-kabinett.

Ben. Vol. V. No. 898. Figure 1107. Val. 453. (Ca. 1650/55). HB. p. 53 and 57.

144

Unidentified biblical scene. (*Potiphar's wife tries to seduce Joseph?*) Genesis 39. v. 7—12. A young woman is trying to prevent a young man from entering (or leaving) a room; at the right a fireplace becomes visible. About 1651/52. Pen and bistre. The form in the right hand side of the sheet may not belong to the main body of the picture. An old vertical fold from the middle is noticeable, as well as two horizontal folds in the top third of the sheet. 180 × 208 mm. Dresden, Kupferstichkabinett.

It would appear that the woman is trying to prevent the youth from leaving the room since he has his hat in his hand and since she is clutching the door post with her right hand behind his back. Hofstede de Groot's interpretation of the Potiphar story seems to be the most likely.

Ben. Vol. V. No. 877a. Figure 1090. Val. 105. (1655/60). HdG. 200. (No date).

145

The holy family. About 1652. Pen and bistre, wash, white body colour. 220×191 mm. Vienna, Albertina.

Ben. Vol. V. No. 888. Figure 1099. Val. 329. (Ca. 1645). HdG. 1412. (Ca. 1645). Rotterdam Catalogue 1956. No. 125. (1645/47).

146

Christ among the doctors. About 1652. Reed pen, some corrections with white body colour; the head of the man above the parapet on the right has been covered with white body colour. 189×252 mm. Paris, Louvre, L. Bonnat Bequest.

Ben. Vol. V. No. 885. Figure 1097. HdG. 686. (No date). Rotterdam Catalogue 1956. No. 206. (1652).

147

Christ appearing as a gardener to the Magdelen. About 1653. Pen and bistre, slightly washed, some white body colour. 192×270 mm. Dresden, Kupferstichkabinett.

Ben. Vol. V. No. 929. Figure 1140. Val. 510. (Ca. 1645). HdG. 226 (Ca. 1637). HB. p. 85.

148

The good samaritan lifting the wounded man from the mule. About 1650/52. Pen and bistre with some corrections in white. 197×205 mm. Weimar, Staatliche Kunstsammlungen.

Ben. Vol. III. No. 615. Figure 747. Val. 377. (Ca. 1650/52). HdG. 519. (No date).

149

The holy family departing for Egypt. About 1652. Reed pen and bistre, slightly washed, corrected with white body colour; the paper has been made up with a strip of paper at the lower right, and a small piece at the lower left. The vegetation in the top left corner has been completely covered with white body colour. The hands of Mary and Joseph were covered with white and have been drawn again. Mary's face has been disfigured by oxidation. Top right, experiments for changing Joseph's arm. 193×241 mm. Berlin, Kupferstichkabinett.

An old copy is in the British Museum. HdG. 880.

Ben. Vol. V. No. 902. Figure 1114. Val. 353. (Ca. 1655). HdG. 53. (No date).

150

Old man praying and angel flying off. (*The imparting of the news of the birth of John the Baptist to his father Zacharias*). About 1655. Reed pen and bistre, changes in the architecture, top left. 199×173 mm. Dresden, Kupferstichkabinett.

The kneeling woman was drawn in later by another hand and is taken from Manoah's offering. Benesch takes this to be the subject of the drawing and feels that it is a project for a new version of a painting of 1641 in the Dresden Gallery (dG. 27. Bredius 509). However, we take the original drawing, without the woman, to be "The Imparting of the news of the birth of John the Baptist to his Father Zacharias" (Luke 1. 8–19). This would give meaning to the temple architecture and the old man's sleepy posture.

Ben. Vol. V. No. 974. Figure 1188. Val. 136. (1641?). HdG. 791. (Ca. 1641).

151

Daniel in the lion's den. (Daniel 6. v. 14–23). About 1652. Reed pen and bistre, wash, some white body colour (partly oxidized). 221×185 mm. Amsterdam, Rijkprentenkabinet, C. Hofstede de Groot bequest.

Rembrandt here made use of the numerous studies of lions which he had done in the years immediately preceding. He enhanced the power and the vigour of the animals to a monumental scale well matching the primitive architecture of the lion's den from whose circular edge the spectators look down as from a cupola. The idea of the interior of the Julius Civilis seems to be foreshadowed here.

Ben. Vol. V. No. 887. Figure 1098. Val. 210. (Ca. 1652). HdG. 1262. (No date). Rotterdam Catalogue 1956. No. 184. (1650/55).

152

A lion lying down, in profile to the right. About 1660/62. Reed pen and bistre. 119×212 mm. Amsterdam, Rijksprentenkabinet.

On the reverse, in an old handwriting: 6 stux leeuwen 3 – g. 26 stux van Rembrant 20 – guld. (6 lions – 3 fl. 26 pieces by Rembrandt 20 fl.).

Ben. Vol. V. No. 1216. Figure 1440. HdG. 1202. (No date).

153

Lioness eating a bird. About 1641. Black chalk, wash in Indian ink, heightened with white on dark brown paper. 127×240 mm. London, British Museum.

Etched by B. Picart, Recueil de Lions, 1728, F. 6 (in reverse).

Ben. Vol. IV. No. 775. Figure 922. HdG. 946. (No date).

154

Elisha makes a piece of iron float on the water. (2 Kings 6. v. 1–7). About 1653. Pen and bistre, wash, rubbed with the finger, on greyish paper. 140×188 mm. The Hague, Bredius Museum.

The strong articulation of the joints of the bodies, especially of the lying man foreshadows Rembrandt's style of figure drawing of the middle of the decade.

Ben. Vol. V. No. 932. Figure 1144. Val. 193. (Ca. 1650). HdG. 1243. (Ca. 1650).

155

Nathan admonishing David. (2 Samuel 12. v. 7–14). About 1654/55. Reed pen and bistre, wash, white body colour. 183×252 mm. New York, Metropolitan Museum of Art.

The present drawing is the maturer of two on the same theme, unsurpassed in colouristic radiancy suggested by the particular technique of reed pen drawing. The "Homer" type of the prophet recurs almost indentically in the figure of the apostle in the background of the painting "Christ and the Woman of Samaria" pf. 1655, dG. 100, Bredius 588. In the figure of David a certain influence of the Indian miniatures copied by Rembrandt at about that time already seems to be apparent.

92 Ben. Vol. V. No. 948. Figure 1159. Val. 168. (Ca. 1663).

156

Susanna and the elders. About 1653. Reed pen and bistre, corrected with white body colour in the figure of Susanna. 175×216 mm. Wroclaw, Ossolineum.

Compare with No. 53.

Ben. Vol. V. No. 928. Figure 1139. HB. p. 85.

157

The reconciliation of Esau and Jacob. (Genesis 33). About 1655. Reed pen and bistre; inscribed by a later hand: Rembrandt. 208×303 mm. Berlin, Kupferstichkabinett.

The doubts expressed by Hofstede de Groot and Lilienfeld were rightly rejected by Valentiner, Rosenberg and Falck. Rosenberg dates this 1650/55. The drawing is a characteristic example of the style of stereometric simplification at its height.

Ben. Vol. V. No. 966. Figure 1180. Val. 85. (Ca. 1650/53). HdG. 17. (No date).

158

The crucifixion. Pen and bistre, on lightly brown toned paper. Oxidized white body colour on the body of Christ. The back of the sitting figure and the bearded rider were drawn in, in a second phase. For this reason the face to the right of the rider was erased with white. (It now shows through, however). Inscribed by a later hand: Rembrandt. 188×235 mm. Weimar, Staatliche Kunstsammlungen.

Ben. Vol. VI. No. C 96. Figure 1637. (Copy). Val. 490. (Ca. 1656). HdG. 520. (No date).

159

God announces his covenant to Abraham. (Genesis 17. v. 1–4). About 1656. Pen and bistre, some white body colour, the upper corners slightly rounded. Dresden, Kupferstichkabinett.

Ben. Vol. V. No. 1003. Figure 1218. Val. 9. (Ca. 1658/60). HdG. 197. (No date).

160

The naming of St. John the Baptist. (Luke 1. v. 11–63). About 1656. Pen and wash in bistre and Indian ink; wash by a later hand; inscribed with a pencil by a later hand: Rembrant. 199×314 mm. Paris, Louvre.

In the Louvre, the present drawing was formerly attributed to the School of Rembrandt (see Hofstede de Groot). The high praise given to the drawing by Schmidt-Degener is justified by the monumentality of the composition. The block like effect of the bedstead closed by the curtains and the table may be compared with the use of similar block forms in Benesch Nos. 1008 and 1009. Whether the washes in Indian ink, particularly those in the background to the right, are entirely by Rembrandt may be queried. This led Benesch to doubt the authenticity of the drawing many years ago as mentioned by Lugt.

Ben. Vol. V. No. 1007. Figure 1219. Val. 272. (Ca. 1655). HdG. 601. (1650/55).

161

Saul and his servants with the Witch of Endor. (I Samuel 28. v. 7–25). About 1657. Pen and bistre, wash, in some places rubbed with the finger. 144×226 mm. The Hague, Bredius Museum.

A copy is at Braunschweig. Rembrandt developed the composition in the present drawing to an unsurpassable clarity and monumental simplicity.

Ben. Vol. V. No. 1028. Figure 1241. Val. 812. (Ca. 1650).

162

Sailing boat driven by the wind. About 1654/55. Pen and bistre, sketch, top in lighter brown. 197×300 mm. Dresden, Kupferstichkabinett.

Benesch entitles this "Christ in the storm on the Sea of Galilee"; in the upper right corner the bust of a frightened Apostle. We are inclined to disagree with this interpretation, (see text page 64).

This is a characteristic example of the geometrically abbreviated style of figure drawing of the middle of the decade which made the figures almost functional mechanisms like articulated dolls.

Ben. Vol. V. No. 954. Figure 1165. Val. 424. (1645). HdG. 219. (Ca. 1633).

163

The angler. About 1654/55. Pen, on brownish paper. Inscribed by a later hand: Rimbrandt. 126×172 mm. Stockholm, National Museum.

The path on the right with the old man walking on it was not done at the same time at the rest of the drawing. In our opinion it was done some time later by another hand.

Ben. Vol. V. No. 1159. Figure 1378. HdG. 1603. (Ca. 1645). Rotterdam Catalogue 1956. No. 196. (1650/55).

164

The return of the prodigal son. About 1656/57. Pen and bistre, wash, corrected with white body colour. Frame line by Rembrandt. 188×272 mm. Dresden, Kupferstichkabinett.

Compare with No. 76.

Ben. Vol. V. No. 1017. Figure 1231. Val. 391. (1655). HdG. 218. (1650/55).

165

The parable of the labourers in the vineyard. About 1660/62. Pen and bistre. 100×142 mm. Leningrad, Hermitage.

Compare with No. 92.

Ben. Vol. V. No. 1055. Figure 1273.

166

Sheet of studies. Old Tobit being led to his son. Painter with easel and seated female model. Tobit study, pen and bistre. Figure in the right of the group erased with white (now shows through the white). Painter (twice) and model, in pen and watery reddish-brown bistre. 195×265 mm. Dresden, Kupferstichkabinett.

Benesch takes this as a sheet of studies for the liberation of St. Peter. This meaning is untenable since the angel (?) accompanying St. Peter (?) has no wings. Besides this, Rembrandt has done this subject many times before and always made his angels recognisable. Valentiner's meaning of "Old Tobit" is undoubtedly the right one. This is further confirmed by the erasing of the figure of the servant (right) who must have appeared too anxious and too much like the main figure. The argument put forward by H. M. Rotermund (Wallraf-Richartz Jahrbuch, Jahrgang XXI 1959) "Mißverstandener Zeichnungen von Rembrandt" p. 173, note 34 is impossible to understand. He says that the Bible makes no reference to a servant. Compare this with the Lutheran version of 'Das Buch Tobias,' Ch. II v. 10. "Und sein blinder Vater stand eilend auf, und eilte, daß er sich stieß. Da rief er *einen Knecht*, der ihn bei der Hand führte, seinem Sohne entgegen." Painter and model: This is a very rare occurence, Rembrandt has used an old sheet with the preliminary sketches of the painter on it, for his new ideas for "Old Tobit." This interpretation by Hofstede de Groot of the "Man in front of the Easel" is undoubtedly right. A fine painting of this subject in the same pose hangs in the Boston Fine Arts Museum. There is probably a difference of about five years between these two studies. (Painter in Front of the Easel, ca. 1658; Tobit with his servant, ca. 1663).

Ben. Vol. V. No. 1062. Figure 1280. (1660/62). Val. 245. (Ca. 1663). HdG. 262. (Ca. 1653).

167

Sheet of studies with an old man being supported by two men walking in front, the figure of the right hand man is repeated; above the group: a young man, and a head of a woman in mourning. About 1655/56. Pen and bistre; inscribed by a later hand: Rimbrandt. 150×125 mm. Weimar, Goethe Nationalmuseum.

The main group contains the ideas that became apparent in an etching "The Three Crosses" (Bartsch 78 1st part). Here we see a helpless old man of St. Peter type being supported by two helpers. The girdles and the swords do not appear in the etching. The woman in the drawing represents the woman sitting on the extreme right of the etching, turned away from the main group of women. The boy looking on does not appear in the etching.

Ben. Vol. V. No. 1000. Figure 1214. HdG. 532. (No date). HB. p. 86. (1652/53).

168

St. Peter at the deathbed of Tabitha. (Acts 9. v. 36—40). About 1622/25. Pen and bistre, some white; frame by Rembrandt. 190×273 mm. Dresden, Kupferstichkabinett.

Rembrandt's style of reed pen drawing appears here in its very latest and most monumental concentration.
Ben. Vol. V. No. 1068. Figure 1286. Val. 540. (Ca. 1660). HdG. 229. (1655/60).

169

Three syndics (De Staalmeester). 1662. Reed pen and bistre, wash, richly applied with white body colour; arched above. 173×205 mm. Berlin, Kupferstichkabinett.
Ben. Vol. V. No. 1178. Figure 1403. Val. 744. (1662). HdG. 101. (Ca. 1661/62).

170

The ark of Noah. About 1659/60. Pen and bistre, wash. 199×243 mm. Chicago, The Art Institute of Chicago.
Ben. Vol. V. No. 1045. Figure 1261. Val. 6. (Ca. 1660). Rotterdam Catalogue 1956. No. 248. (1655/62).

171

Diana and Actaeon. (Ovid: Metamorphosis, III 131–252). About 1662–65. Pen and bistre, wash, white body colour on grey brown paper. The white body colour has deteriorated and the original work shows through. The dog to the right of Actaeon was erased and the dog, front right, inserted later. The dark half figure in the middle of the drawing was erased but due to oxidation it is now particularly noticeable. Dresden, Kupferstichkabinett.
Compare with text page 68.
Ben. Vol. V. No. 1210. Figure 1434. Val. 600 (Ca. 1660). HdG. 240. (Ca. 1660).

172

The conspiracy of Julius Civilis. (Tacitus: Historae 1. 59. IV, 13–15). About 1660/61. Pen and bistre, wash, some white body colour; arched above. 196×180 mm. Munich, Graphische Sammlung.
On the reverse of the drawing, an announcement of the funeral of Rebecca de Vos, October 25th, 1661. Preparatory drawing for the painting in the City Hall of Amsterdam, now in the Stockholm Nationalmuseum, dG. 225, Bredius 482. Only very few alterations in the drawing occur (the head of the man standing before the table, the figure of his seated neighbour and Civilis' headgear are drawn twice). The sentiments decisively contradict Bauch's opinion that it is a sketch made to commemorate the complete painting before its mutilation.
Ben. Vol. V. No. 1061. Figure 1279. Val. 588. (1660/61.) HdG. 409. (No date).

173

A lady riding out, hawking. About 1662/65. Pen and bistre; the composition is arched above by a semi-circle, drawn with a compass; redrawn probably by another hand in red chalk, also the border line. 214×245mm. Dresden, Kupferstichkabinett.
At the right, first a horse in profile was drawn with slight pen lines. Afterwards it was covered with vigourous reed pen strokes representing the man on horseback who follows the lady rider. On the reverse is a sketch for a double portrait in a large frame.
Ben. Vol. V. No. 1183. Figure 1404. Val. 784a. (Ca. 1665). HdG. 260. (Later period).

174

The presentation in the temple. (Luke 2. v. 25–32). Signed and dated: Rembrandt f. 1661. Pen and brush in bistre. White body colour, arched above. 120×89 mm. The Hague, Royal Library.
Drawing in the album of Dr. Jacobus Heyblock, Minister of the Dutch Church. Rembrandt attempted to give in the present drawing the illusion of a little painting closed in its frame, by adopting a combination of brush and pen, together with scraping in and body colour. It is, of his late drawings, the one which approaches the technical structure of contemporary paintings most closely. Although there cannot be talk of a graphic system in the present drawing as it is still maintained in other contemporary drawings, the transformation of Rembrandt's handwriting into artistic form is so immediate and overwhelming that it is difficult to mention a painting which would surpass the little drawing in transfigured spiritual grandeur.
Ben. Vol. V. No. 1057. Figure 1275. Val. 318. HdG. 1241. Rotterdam Catalogue 1956. No. 250.

The Plates

A-B

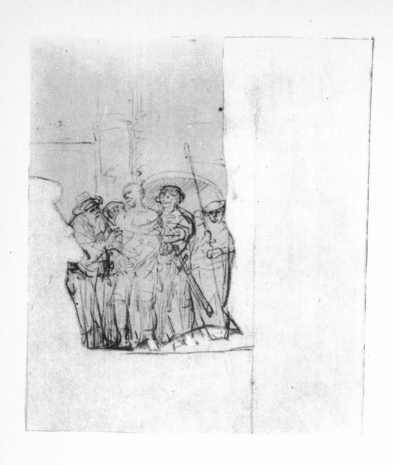

C-E

Van Segen

7

13

14

17

Drommedaris.
Rembrandt ferit.
·633·
Amsterdam.

65.

Rembrandt

23

24

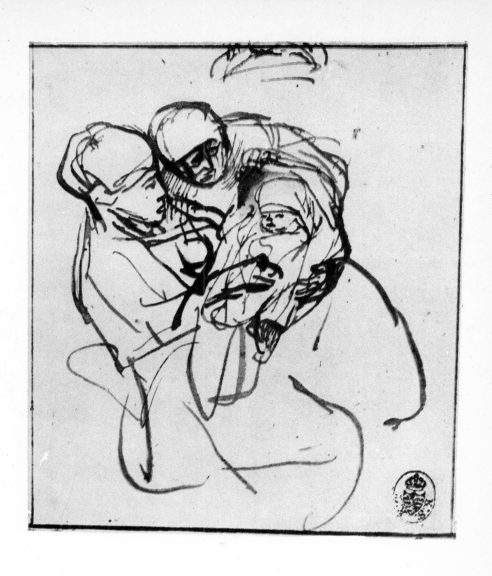

28

40

43

44

46

48

55

Rembrand van Ryn

Λ

60

63

Rembrant

74

78

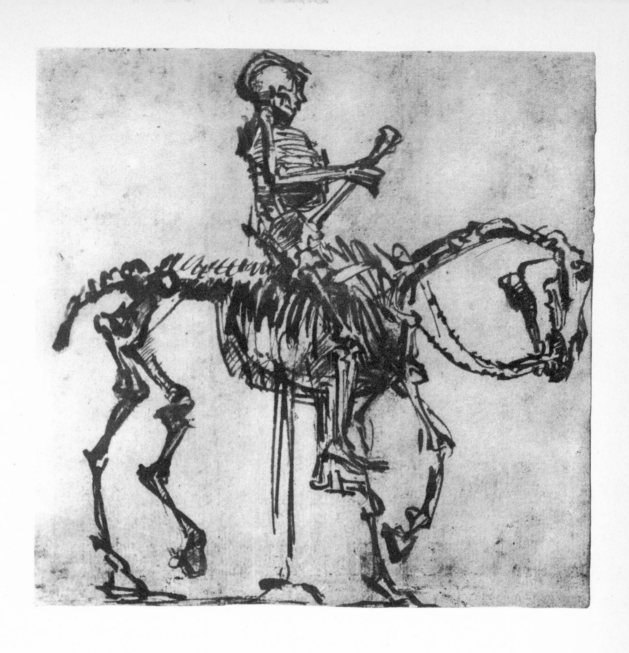

82

Rembrandt

85

88

92

98

geteken door Rembrant van Rhijn naer hijn selver
soo als hij in hijn schilderkamer gekleet was:

138

143

146

154

166

168

169

173

Bauch, Kurt: Die Kunst des jungen Rembrandt, Heidelberg 1933.

Bauch, Kurt: Rembrandt und Lievens. Wallraf-Richartz-Jahrbuch XI, 1939, p. 239.

Bauch, Kurt: Der frühe Rembrandt und seine Zeit, Berlin (1960).

Benesch, Otto: Die Zeichnungen des Budapester Museums der schönen Künste. Belvedere VII, 1925, p. 119.

Benesch, Otto: Rembrandt; Werk und Forschung, Vienna 1935.

Benesch, Otto: The Drawings of Rembrandt. Vol. I–VI, London (1954/1957).

Benesch, Otto: Rembrandt as a draughtsman, London (1960).

Floerke, Gustav: Studien zur niederländischen Kunst und Kulturgeschichte, Munich 1905.

Fraenger, Wilhelm: Der junge Rembrandt, Heidelberg 1920.

Hamann, Richard: Rembrandt, Potsdam (1948).

Hanfstaengel, Eberhard: Rembrandt, III Edition, Munich 1958.

Hauser, Arnold: Sozialgeschichte der Kunst und Literatur, Munich 1958.

Henkel, M. D.: Catalogus van de Nederlandsche Teekeningen in het Rijksmuseum te Amsterdam, I: Rembrandt en zijn school, s'Gravenhage 1942.

Hofstede de Groot, Cornelis: Die Urkunden über Rembrandt (Quellenstudien zur holländischen Kunstgeschichte, Vol. III), The Hague 1906.

Huizinga, J.: Holländische Kultur des 17. Jahrhunderts, Jena 1933.

Jahn, Johannes: Rembrandt, Leipzig 1958.

Kauffmann, Hans: Zur Kritik der Rembrandt-Zeichnungen. Repertorium für Kunstwissenschaft, Vol. 47, 1926, p. 157.

Koot, Ton: Rembrandt und seine Nachtwache, Amsterdam 1954.

Kries, Ernst und Kunz, Otto: Die Legende vom Künstler, Vienna 1934.

Leporini, Heinrich: Künstlerzeichnung (Bibliothek für Kunst und Antiquitätensammler, Vol. 30) Berlin 1928.

Leporini, Heinrich: Handzeichnungen großer Meister: Rembrandt, Berlin (1926).

Lugt, Frits: Mit Rembrandt in Amsterdam, Berlin 1920.

Münz, Ludwig: Die Kunst Rembrandts und Goethes Sehen, Leipzig 1934.

Münz, Ludwig: Rembrandts Altersstil. Jahrbuch der Kunsthistorischen Sammlungen in Wien. N.F. IX, 1935, p. 183.

Münz, Ludwig: Rembrandt: Etchings, London (1952).

Neumann, Carl: Aus der Werkstatt Rembrandts (Heidelberger kunsthistorische Abhandlungen, Vol. III), Heidelberg 1918.

Neumann, Carl: Rembrandt Handzeichnungen, Munich 1918.

Neumann, Carl: Rembrandt. III Edition, Munich 1922.

Nordenfalk, Carl: (Introduction to) Rembrandt, Catalogue of the Exhibition in the National Museum in Stockholm 1956.

Riegl, Alois: Das holländische Gruppenportrait, Vienna 1931.

Saxl, Fritz: Rembrandt's Manoah's sacrifice. Studies of the Warburg Institute IX, London 1939.

Schmidt, Heinrich: Rembrandt als Dramatiker. Jahrbuch der Staatlichen Kunstakademie Düsseldorf 1948/50, p. 166.

Schmidt, Heinrich: Rembrandt, der islamitische Orient und die Antike. Festschrift für Ernst Kühnel, Berlin 1959, p. 336.

Schmidt-Degener, F.: Dessin hollandais de Jerome Bosch a Rembrandt. Catalogue of the exhibition, Brussels 1937/38.

Schmidt-Degener, F.: Rembrandt und das holländische Barock. Studien der Bibliothek Warburg IX, Leipzig 1928.

Schneider, H.: Ferdinand Bol als Monumentalmaler im Amsterdamer Rathaus. Jahrbuch der preußischen Kunstsammlungen Vol. 47, 1926, p. 73.

Slive, Seymour: Rembrandt and his Critics, 1630–1730. The Hague 1953.

Valentiner, Wilhelm: Rembrandt und seine Umgebung, Strasbourg 1905.

Valentiner, Wilhelm: Aus Rembrandts Häuslichkeit. Jahrbuch für Kunstwissenschaft, Vol. I, 1923, p. 277.

Valentiner, Wilhelm: Komödiantendarstellungen Rembrandts. Zeitschrift für bildende Kunst, Vol. 59, 1925/26,
p. 265.

Valentiner, Wilhelm: Rembrandt Zeichnungen. Vol. I, Stuttgart (1925). Vol. II, Stuttgart (1933).

Valentiner, Wilhelm: Rembrandt und Spinoza, London 1957.

"Wie war Rembrandt?" Weekblad O.K.W., Mededlingen 1956.

Amsterdam, Rijkmuseum: 79, 89, 125, 126, 127, 142, 151, 152.

Amsterdam, Rembrandt House: 131.

Berlin (formerly), The State Museum: 2, 24, 30, 32, 51, 72, 75, 80, 106, 149, 157, 169.

Bremen, Kunsthalle: 20.

Budapest, Museum of Fine Arts: 10, 22, 23, 34, 117, 118, 120, 122.

Chatsworth Settlement: 102, 103.

Chicago, The Art Institute: 137, 170.

Constance, Jeannine le Brun: 67, 88, 104.

Copenhagen, Royal Engravings Collection: 31.

Darmstadt, Hessisches Landesmuseum: 81, 126a.

Dresden, State Photographic Library: 3, 4, 6, 7, 9, 11, 12, 17, 25, 27, 33, 44, 53, 55, 57, 58, 74, 78, 100, 119, 130, 134, 136, 143, 144, 147, 150, 162, 164, 166, 168, 171, 173.

Dresden, Engravings department of the State Art Collection: 129, 140, 159.

Groningen, Fotobedrijf: 54, 84.

Haarlem, Teyler Museum: 76, 99.

Hamburg, Kleinhempel-Kunsthalle: 52.

Hannover, Private Collection: 70.

Leipzig, Museum of Pictorial Art: 14, 46.

Leningrad, State Hermitage: 5, 105, 112, 113, 165.

London, British Museum: 1, 43, 48, 63, 66, 71, 87, 97, 108, 132, 133, 138, 153.

Munich, State Graphic Art Collection: 123, 128, 172.

Naples, Soperintendenza alle Gallerie: 141.

New York, The Pierpont Morgan Library: 26, 29, 47, 93.

New York, Metropolitan Museum: 121, 155.

Oxford, Ashmolean Museum: 124.

Paris, Departement des estampes, Louvre: 69, 94, 95, 101, 146, 160.

Paris, Archives photographiques: 96.

Paris, Private Collection: 110.

Rotterdam, Museum Boymans van Beuningen: 92, 139.

Stockholm, National Museum: 35, 36, 135, 163.

The Hague, Royal Library: 174.

The Hague, Dienst voor schone Kunsten: 154, 161.

The Hague, A. Frequin: 77.

Venice, Foto Rossi: 13.

Vienna, Albertina: 61, 90, 91, 109, 115, 145.

Warsaw, Engravings department of the University Library: 15, 64, 65, 83, 85, 86, 116.

Weimar, Nationale Forschungs- und Gedenkstätten: 16, 19, 37, 40, 167.

Weimar, Photo archives of the State Art Collection: 18, 21, 39, 41, 42, 45, 49, 60, 82, 111, 114, 125a, 148, 158.

Wroclaw, Ossolineum: 8, 28, 38, 50, 56, 59, 62, 73, 107, 156.